Studies in European Politics

This series provides brief and up-to-date analyses of European political issues, including developments in the European Community and in transnational political forces, and also major problems in particular European countries. The research is undertaken by the European Centre for Political Studies, established in 1978 at the Policy Studies Institute with the sponsorship of the European Cultural Foundation. The series is edited by the Head of the Centre, Dr Roger Morgan.

Studies scheduled for publication in 1979 include:

1. The Future of the European Parliament, *David Coombes*.
2. Towards Transnational Parties in the European Community, *Geoffrey & Pippa Pridham*.
3. European Integration, Regional Devolution and National Parliaments, *D. Coombes, L. Condorelli, R. Hrbek, W. Parsons, S. Schüttemeyer*.
4. Eurocommunism: the Foreign Policy Dimensions, *Carole Webb*.
5. Liberalism .in the European Community, *Ove Guldberg and Niels Haagerup*.
6. Social Democracy in the European Community, *Norbert Gresch*.
7. Political Forces in Spain, Greece and Portugal, *Beate Kohler*.
8. Parliament and the Economy in Four West European Countries, *G. Amato, A. Dupas, J. Kooiman, S. Walkland*.

Of related interest:

Westminster and Devolution, *Study of Parliament Group in association with PSI*.

The Future
of the
European Parliament

David Coombes

Studies in European Politics 1

Acknowledgements

The author is indebted to a number of individuals and organisations who contributed in different ways to this study. In particular, special thanks are due to the European Cultural Foundation who gave a generous grant to the European Centre for Political Studies at PSI to enable the study to be undertaken. The author would also like to express his appreciation of the help given by the Committee of Co-operation for European Parliamentary Studies; much of the content of the study, and especially that of Chapter IV was based on conversations and discussions with the Committee's members, and on the Committee's seminars and other research activities since its foundation in 1975. The expert guidance and help given by members and officials of the European Parliament and officials of the Commission of the European Communities are also gratefully acknowledged; special thanks are extended to those who kindly read and commented on earlier drafts of the manuscript. Needless to say, any errors or omissions which remain are solely the author's responsibility.

C

ISBN 0–85374–168–9

Published by PSI, 1-2 Castle Lane, London SW1E 6DR
Printed by George Berridge & Co. Ltd., London & Thetford

Contents

I The Significance of the European Parliament

The background to the study

The first election of a European Parliament by direct universal suffrage in June 1979 will bring that institution to the public's attention much more than ever before. The election is in itself an event of great political curiosity, and potentially of great political importance. It represents the achievement of many years of political struggle within the European Community to introduce European elections in accordance with the founding treaties.

However, the present study is not about the European election itself. Doubtless there will be many studies in the next few years of the election campaign and its results. Our concern here is with the more persistent and complicated question of the future role of the European Parliament as an institution. That question has an obvious bearing on the election and could be one of the issues in it. But the Parliament's political significance is not due only to the holding of direct elections.

Indeed one problem for the voters themselves will be to understand what sort of body they are electing. By the standards of any free election, but especially of national elections in Western Europe, the first election of the European Parliament will take place in unfamiliar and confusing circumstances. The European Parliament will have impinged very little, if at all, on people's lives up to now. It is difficult to make out a case on the basis of its present role that it will be likely to do so much more in the foreseeable future. Indeed, what must be especially perplexing for many voters is the fact that some of the national governments in the Community have come out strongly—even as a condition of agreeing to holding an election at all—against any future increase in the European Parliament's power. Does not that suggest that such a body is hardly worth voting for, let alone writing a book about?

In fact, the voters need have no illusions: there is not much even the British and French governments can do on their own to stop the European Parliament exercising significant political power in future under certain conditions. Not only do particular governments come and go; they are also forced to moderate their attitudes from time to time when they can get what they want only by co-operation with others as is the case in the Community. In other words, no one can predict how the governments of Member States will view the role of the Euro-

1

pean Parliament in future in the light of changing circumstances. Secondly, the very holding of a direct election endows the Parliament with political authority and that is precisely why it has been resisted. Thirdly, by far the most important reason why the future development of the European Parliament is a live issue is that the Parliament's power is not the same thing as the sum of its formal powers granted by the Community treaties or by amendments to them. As I shall try to show in Chapter II even its present potential is far greater than is usually supposed. Indeed the standing, influence and impact of any parliament never depend only on its formal powers defined in a strictly legal sense. (If they did the British Parliament would be a far more powerful body than it is today.) Much of this book will be concerned with exactly how parliaments obtain and exercise power in different circumstances and with different results. One conclusion will be that there are plenty of opportunities for the European Parliament to become a more important body with much greater impact on people's lives.

I shall go further than this and argue that only by strengthening the European Parliament in ways I shall describe can the Community be subjected to principles of parliamentary democracy. What I have to say, therefore, is relevant regardless of 'pro-European' or 'anti-European' views. It is not intended as a defence of the European Community, or even as an argument for European integration. I start from the assumption that both Europe and the Community are there and will not go away, so that something has to be done about them. The real significance of the European elections is what they might contribute to developing parliamentary democracy in the Community.

However, simply holding elections will not solve the problem of providing parliamentary democracy. One reason for this study, therefore, is to encourage a more rigorous and better-informed public discussion of the European Parliament that the introduction of direct elections makes urgent. An increasing number of books on the Parliament have appeared recently. But, while giving a lot of useful information and comment, especially about the circumstances of the European election itself, they have tended to take one of two perspectives: either what the Parliament means for the Community, or what it means for parliamentary democracy.[1] Here I shall treat those perspectives as inseparable. The future of the Parliament (and for that matter of the Community itself) is not relevant only from the point of view of European integration. And, as if the question of parliamentary democracy were not complicated enough already (given the doubts we have about it at the present time in all parliamentary democracies), in relation to the Community it is further confused by all sorts of issues that need careful disentangling.

The election will be seen by many to open up new opportunities for the Parliament to assert itself. But again there is a risk that arguments will get

---

[1] For example, John Fitzmaurice, *The European Parliament*, (London, 1978) and *The Party Groups in the European Parliament*, (London, 1975); V. Herman and J. Lodge, *The European Parliament and the European Community*, (London, 1978); R. Jackson, *The Powers of the European Parliament*, (London, 1977); Institut d'Études Juridiques Européennes, *Le Parlement Européen: Pouvoir, Élection, Rôle futur*, (Liège, 1976); C. Sasse et al., *Decision making in the European Community*, (London, 1977), pp. 243–352.

confused and confusing, both in relation to the nature and purposes of the Community and to those of parliamentary democracy. For one thing the Community is in political terms *sui generis*, which means that the arguments about the Parliament's future role cannot just be the same arguments as those used about parliamentary institutions elsewhere. For another thing there is a sense in which nothing is *sui generis*, so that people must argue inevitably in language and ideas derived from their experience of previous and existing political institutions.

In the remainder of this chapter I shall seek to explain briefly why the introduction of direct elections is less important than the role of the Parliament itself, and then try equally briefly to dispel suspicions that the Parliament is not the best way to provide greater democracy in the Community. I shall also outline a problem that much of the rest of the book will seek to solve, namely, that people who want to strengthen the Parliament have different reasons for doing so. In Chapter II, I shall try to explain the main constraints on the Parliament's role up to now, given that these have not all arisen from the way its members are selected, and I shall consider its existing potential for future development. In Chapter III, I shall ask precisely why parliamentary democracy should be considered relevant to the Community, whether or not we like the Community as it is, and my argument that the Community needs a strengthened Parliament will be set out there. In Chapter IV, I shall tackle the question of what a strengthened Parliament could mean in terms of our ideas and principles of parliamentary democracy and look for models of what sort of parliament should be envisaged, asking in particular how we can improve on past mistakes and disappointments in national experience. Finally, in Chapter V, I shall suggest how the European Parliament might be strengthened, in ways that both the nature and purposes of the Community, as well as the need for more effective democratic institutions, demand.

The significance of direct elections

Of course one reason why we have to look beyond the election in June 1979 is that the Decision of 20 September 1976 did not provide just for one direct election but for direct elections.[2] In other words the very nature of the European Parliament is to some extent transformed in that it becomes a directly elected body. That is bound to increase its democratic legitimacy, as opponents of direct elections have been right to point out. Given what we know about free elections and political representation—in particular that people do not vote spontaneously but under all sorts of influences including those arising from the nature of the regime concerned and the political organisations within it—people, and politicians in particular, are wrong to put so much a gloss on the moral effect of being elected as they usually do in relation to the European Parliament. At least, however, there is some moral gain. It is difficult to pin down what that means in legal, let alone material, terms and I shall not try to do so now.[3] But even so it is

---

[2] The Decision, taken by the Council, is published officially in *Official Journal of the European Communities*, L278 of 8.10.1976.

[3] For a useful discussion with relevant citations, see Herman and Lodge, *op. cit.*, pp. 73–93.

widely agreed that electing the members of the Parliament by universal suffrage, instead of having them nominated by national parliaments, will make a significant difference to the institution's authority.

In that sense, however, (and in practical ways that I shall deal with in a moment) it will not be until elections are held according to a uniform electoral procedure, as provided by the Decision of 20 September, that the full effects of being directly elected will be seen.[4] The Decision and its implementation so far have been the result of a hard fought compromise and many qualifications apply at least for the first election.[5] Above all, as the Decision states in article 7.2, 'the electoral procedure shall be governed in each Member State by its national provisions'. Not only such a fundamental question as the type of electoral system, and also therefore that of the nature of constituencies, has been determined at national level, but also all sorts of important aspects of holding elections such as the entitlement to vote, eligibility for election, nomination of candidates, filling of vacancies as they arise, rules governing the campaign and validation of results.[6] In fact, electoral systems and constituencies apart, the variety in procedures adopted does not seem as if it will be all that great (or so very different from customary national practice). However, while five Member States have decided to organise the election on the basis of single national lists (two of them with qualifications to take account of regional factors), the other four have created regional or local constituencies. All but Britain will use a system of proportional representation but the consequences of that exception could have a serious effect on the overall result and the representation of British members.[7] All in all, although the election will be held during the same period of days and the results will be announced together, and although Community institutions and organisations will do their best to highlight European issues in the campaign, the election will for the vast majority of voters be a special form of State election rather than a genuinely European one. Even where regional constituencies have been adopted, members of the Parliament will be representing to a large extent different Member States on a State basis.

One major reason for that would exist even if a uniform procedure had been adopted; it is the absence of truly European political parties, with the sort of organisations that are so crucial to free elections at least in this part of the world, if not everywhere. That is also a major reason why the voters are likely to be ill-informed and confused, since, though European federations of some parties have been formed and will be active, it is national party organisations that will be

---

[4] Article 7.1 provides that, pursuant to the relevant articles in the original Community treaties, 'the Assembly shall draw up a proposal for a uniform electoral procedure'.

[5] For an account of the recent history, see Fitzmaurice, *op. cit.*, 1978, pp. 51–89. See also European Parliament, *Elections to the European Parliament by direct universal suffrage*, (Luxembourg, July 1977).

[6] Fitzmaurice, loc. cit. For the various national provisions, see, European Parliament, *National Electoral Laws on Direct Elections*, series published by the Directorate-General for Research & Documentation, (Luxembourg).

[7] Fitzmaurice, *op. cit.*, 1978, pp. 84–86 and 134–7. For details of the different national systems, see European Parliament, *Laws (or Draft Legislation) for Direct Elections to the European Parliament: a comparative survey*, (Luxembourg, 24 August 1978), P.E.54.676.

dominant, in spite of the fact that the successful candidates will be returned to an institution that so far has operated with transnational political groups (as will be explained later).[8] The problems thus created for the electorate could cause high abstention, or a result the meaning of which is even more questionable than that of ordinary elections, or both. Moreover, although the Community is far more than an ordinary international organisation, it has no central government with a record or programme that people can vote for or against. That might not make such a very great difference in all the States but it is intensified as a source of confusion by the fact that everywhere the very decisions about electoral procedure have involved difficult compromises internally among political and other forces relevant mainly at a State level, and the campaigns (for they will be various) will undoubtedly involve the same sort of thing.[9]

Just how much all this matters for the European Parliament's future role I shall finally consider in Chapter V. However, there are clearly reasons for suspecting that the holding of a direct election in this qualified form, and at this stage of the Community's development, might reduce the Parliament's authority as well as increase it. Those who have campaigned for the introduction of direct elections so stalwartly since 1974, when the question became a practical one again, did so for two main reasons. It was seen as the only way of breaking the vicious circle the French governments of Gaullist persuasion had forced the Parliament into—no powers without elections, but no elections without powers. Once the State governments seemed more or less ready at least to reconsider their collective position on direct elections, then it was time to jump. Secondly, the system of nomination created impossible problems of a practical nature which direct election should overcome. At least it will mean that the membership is doubled and that members have the opportunity to be full time and to serve a fixed term of five years. But it is nevertheless a risky sort of achievement and makes the general question of the Parliament's role all the more important to understand.

The real problem, therefore, is to understand what sort of political system it is to which the European Parliament belongs. If there is no central government, if the Community is the result essentially of international treaties designed mainly to set up a common market, and if there are no real political parties, then what is the purpose of electing a body called a parliament in such a system? Indeed, the official nomenclature in Britain still calls it an 'Assembly', as if to follow the rhetoric of that question.

In fact, the best reason for using the term 'Parliament' (as I shall do throughout this book) is to avoid confusion (that invariably arises in Britain) with other international assemblies in Europe—in particular the Parliamentary Assembly of the Council of Europe, whose premises in Strasbourg the European Parliament often uses for its sittings. But that is itself significant because, although the Community is not a federation of states with its own government, it is neverthe-

---

[8] On European party federations and political groups in the European Parliament, see pp. 30–32 and 104–8.

[9] Fitżmaurice, *op. cit.*, 1978, pp. 58–87.

less quite different from other European organisations, as should by now be generally understood even in the new Member States.

The treaties provide the framework of a kind of written constitution in two especially important ways: by establishing the Community Institutions (the Parliament, Council, Commission, Court of Justice) with their own corporate identity separate from the Member States; and by endowing those Institutions with powers in their own right to make law that is directly binding on and within the States.[10] These characteristics have caused the Community to be distinguished as a 'supranational' organisation. That term was not approved by all the founders of the Community[11] but it does serve to describe the special quality of the legal and indeed political, authority that the Community has been given to exercise in its own right. I shall continue to use it here to describe that quality.

As I shall argue in Chapter III, it is not only because the Community is supranational that the role of parliamentary democracy is important in relation to it. Indeed, one reason for setting it up with that sort of constitutional framework was to take account of such things as the rule of law and public accountability that we claim to be so important in the States themselves. Traditional diplomacy and other types of international organisation were thought to respect those conditions far too little, if at all. I must not allow this explanation to run on too far at this point, because it is the subject matter mainly of Chapter III. However, since many people have questioned the need for a European Parliament at all on democratic grounds, these grounds need spelling out.

The European Parliament and democracy
Some have argued persistently since the Community's beginnings that a reinforcement of the Parliament, by directly electing it and increasing its power, is essential, if the Community is to function with anything like adequate democracy.

One weakness of this argument, however, is that there is a strong counter argument that draws no less on democratic principles. This counter argument is that the best, if not the only proper, way to provide democracy in the Community is to preserve, or even to strengthen, the power of the governments of Member

---

[10] There are still strictly speaking three Communities each based on a separate treaty (the European Coal and Steel Community, founded in 1952, the European Atomic Energy Community and the European Economic Community, both founded in 1957). I shall use throughout the term 'Community' to refer to all three Communities in their common aspects, but all treaty references will be to the Treaty establishing the Economic Community (EEC Treaty). The European Parliament was established as the Assembly of the Coal and Steel Community in 1952 but acted for the other two Communities when they were established (as did the Court). The Commission consists of 13 members appointed by the Member States' governments, but acts independently; it has various functions of an executive nature, including the duty to propose legislative measures as provided by the treaties to the Council for decision and to defend its proposals before the Council, as well as enacting some measures on its own. The Council consists of ministers representing the States' governments and is at present the body responsible for enacting most Community law and making most Community policy. The role of the Institutions will be discussed in Chapter III.

[11] See Jean Monnet, *Mémoires*, (Paris 1976), pp. 352; Walter Hallstein, *Europe in the Making*, (London, 1972), p.39

States in the Community's institutional system. The crucial assumption here is that the State governments are democratically accountable through national parliaments and by other means within the States themselves. So, the argument runs, it is the Council, where these democratic governments are directly represented and not the European Parliament that should be seen as the truly democratic organ at Community level. If the Parliament's power were increased, especially over the Community's right to make law, it could only be at the expense of the Council's power and at the same time, therefore, of the democratically elected State governments and parliaments.

Opposition to developing the European Parliament (including its direct election) is currently strong among a disparate collection of political forces including mainly the British Labour Party and nationalist parties, various Danish political groupings, and French Gaullists and Communists. The one thing they tend to have in common is a general suspicion of the supranational character of the Community. To a large extent what is opposed is not the development of the European Parliament so much as that of the Community itself. If the argument is that only existing national institutions can ever provide effective democracy, then this opposition both to a stronger European Parliament and to a stronger Community would seem to be logical. Such an extreme view of the desirability and indivisibility of national sovereignty is not often made explicit, however, though it is in some right wing attacks on the Community, for example those of Mr. Enoch Powell in England or of M. Michel Debré in France.[12] For those who take this extreme view the issue is fairly clear: the Community approach was wrong from the very start. The question becomes what type of international co-operation, if any, is to be preferred on democratic grounds. Some loss of power for national parliaments is inevitable given that the Community's supranational powers make it necessary to delegate legislative powers to ministers acting in the Council. It is also partly inevitable, however, given the difficulties encountered in holding ministers accountable for their participation in international negotiations of any kind, conducted as these usually have to be in private and on the basis of bargaining and compromise. Sometimes opposition to the European Parliament is simply opposition to any kind of international co-operation. Sometimes it is simply a defence of traditional forms of diplomacy which are hardly very desirable on democratic grounds.

Suspicion of the European Parliament is certainly not confined, however, to those opposed to the Community or its development. For example, Andrew Shonfield, in his widely-quoted Reith Lectures of 1972, foresaw conflict between a strengthened European Parliament on the one hand and the parliaments of Member States on the other and considered this a threat to the Community's future development. He maintained that the existing national parliaments were far more effective in providing democratic legitimacy than the European Parliament could be in the foreseeable future, especially in what he chose to call the

---

[12] See, for example, House of Lords, Select Committee on the European Communities, Session 1977/78, 44th Report, HL 256–II pp. 186–7; *Le Monde*, 1 July 1978, p. 1.

'older democracies in the north of Europe, led by Britain'. In order to strengthen the Community's democratic legitimacy, Shonfield went on to propose means of involving the national parliaments more directly in the Community's legislative process. His outline scheme for co-ordinating national legislative activity, rather than 'imposing' legislation from a Community level, envisaged the European Parliament acting as a sort of 'committee of committees' at the centre of a network of parallel committees in the national parliaments acting 'in unison'.[13]

One practical obstacle to such a scheme is that parliaments of Member States do not have the same powers, procedures and organisations; they do not all even have specialised legislative committees and often for fundamental reasons. The organisation and the behaviour of a national parliament are determined largely by the internal political system—both in the longer term structural sense and in terms of the prevailing political circumstances (such as the relative strength of the different political parties and so on). The degree of uniformity in national parliaments on which Shonfield's sort of proposal really depends would imply a blending of existing national differences that is not actually demanded by the treaties, or envisaged in any explicit view of the Community's development so far and certainly not by those who wish to strengthen the European Parliament.

If, however, the national parliaments are to provide democratic influence and control through the Council, then we face the insuperable problem that the Council does not represent directly the people living in the Member States. It represents the existing governments at State level, and therefore the party or parties currently in office, whereas within a particular Member State one might expect some diversity in the reactions to any particular Community matter, given the internal differences that exist among political parties, among regions and among social and economic groups. It is meant to be a characteristic of pluralist democracies, after all, that these differences should find expression in institutions capable of influencing and controlling government. Can representation indirectly at an international level through a body like the Community's Council ensure adequate expression of the diversity of opinions, demands and interests that are found within regimes like those of the Community's Member States?

In the Benelux countries, Italy, and the Federal Republic of Germany the reaction to the effects of Community membership on democracy has usually been to campaign for a more effective European Parliament as a means of compensating for the loss of power of national parliaments. However, in all the States now there are some procedures for enabling ministers to consult their own parliament before agreeing to important measures in the Community.[14] The role of the State parliament in Community business ultimately depends in all the Member States on its relationship with the executive (and therefore on the nature of the regime concerned).[15] Even where the executive is conventionally subject to extensive influence and control by parliament (and that cannot be said

---

[13] A. Shonfield, *Europe: Journey to an Unknown Destination*, (London, 1973), pp. 69–82.
[14] The best account so far is in Fitzmaurice, *op. cit.*, 1975, and *op. cit.*, 1978, pp. 27–51. See also Sasse, *op. cit.*, pp. 42–66.
[15] Fitzmaurice, loc. cit., 1978; Sasse, *op. cit.*, pp. 42–66.

8

of Britain and the French Fifth Republic), a consequence of the Community is that substantial power has to be delegated to ministers and their officials, who require wide discretion in order to participate effectively in Community decision making. Although not always so intellectually dishonest as it sounds, the view that State parliaments rather than the European Parliament should provide democracy in the Community, becomes nothing more in effect than a defence of the power of the government within the State concerned. The democratic grounds of such a view are invariably suspect on closer examination.

Indeed, it is not just the Community that challenges the power of State parliaments. There already exists within all the Member States a tendency to consider parliament as an inadequate means of representation in modern government. That is of course no reason for allowing membership of the Community to make parliaments even more inadequate. But it does mean that it is not enough simply to fall back on a defence of the privileges (such as they are) of existing parliaments.

One extremely important consequence of the transfer of certain legislative powers to a Community level has been the development of European organisations representing private social and economic interests seeking to exert influence directly at a Community level. There is evidence that, even in a new Member State like Britain, groups such as farmers' organisations, trade and employers' associations, and professional bodies react to the Community not by regretting the effects on the State parliament but by taking immediate advantage of direct means of access to a Community level (for example, formal consultation, lobbying of the Commission, the Council and the European Parliament, and representation through the Economic and Social Committee). Direct access whether of an official, consultative nature or of an informal, lobbying variety has even extended to forms of public authority within the Member States but not integrated with central government itself, such as semi-autonomous public corporations and other agencies, and in particular local authorities and regional governments.[16] These developments are evidence that Member States' boundaries fail to circumscribe certain common interests directly affected by Community decisions (such as those of farmers, workers, employers, particular industries, local and regional communities, and even ethnic and political minorities).

This seemingly inevitable consequence of the Community threatens to strengthen the power of private organised groups to by-pass parliamentary means, unless such parliamentary means are created in an effective manner at the level of the Community. It underlines the need for a parliamentary body at that level to aggregate and integrate special interests by-passing national parliaments into policies designed to serve the common interest. In an international organisation of the Community's type the differences that have to be recognised and reconciled are not only those among State governments but also those among political, social, economic, regional and other interests.

---

[16] For the UK, see Hansard Society for Parliamentary Government, *The British People: Their Voice in Europe*, (London, 1977).

The question remains, however, whether these and other factors weakening the role of State parliaments are not the consequences only of the supranational nature of the Community. If they are, then would it not be better, at least from the point of view of democracy, to find some other method of organising the Community? That is indeed what some of the State governments, political groupings in the States, and a number of academic and other commentators, have suggested. In fact, the recent development of the Community into new spheres such as monetary and, to some extent, economic policy, as well as foreign policy, has actually been accompanied by a dilution of the supranational principle as I shall explain in Chapter III. The question of the European Parliament's role as a contribution to democracy cannot be considered, therefore, unless we first take account of the political needs of the Community itself. We cannot just take it for granted that strengthening the European Parliament is the way to make the Community democratic. If the real aim is to reinforce parliamentary institutions, then perhaps the Community itself should be made to develop into a different type of organisation.

The European Parliament and the future of the Community

It is essential to see the future of the European Parliament in relation to that of the Community for another reason. Much of the support for a stronger Parliament is based, not only on democratic grounds but on a view of the Parliament, 'as an instrument by which the Community can be dynamised'.[17] In other words, there is what might be called a *utilitarian* as well as a purely *democratic* view from which the Parliament's future can be judged.

There is a strong hint of this view in the one major, independent review of the Parliament's role to have been made from a Community level (albeit before direct elections were introduced)—that of the so-called Vedel Group in 1972.[18] While the Group's report stressed both 'democracy' and 'efficiency' as grounds for increasing the Parliament's powers, its general theme (to which I shall return in context later)[19] was that a stronger Parliament would be a means of restoring the institutional balance between the general, European interest and the special, State interests in such a way as to renew the dynamic in Community decision making allegedly lost since the establishment of the Common Market (in 1969) if not earlier in the crisis of 1965. To a large extent the strengthened Parliament was seen in the Vedel Report as a means of giving political support to the Commission in its role as mediator among the governments. Indeed, throughout much of the campaign for raising the Parliament's status by direct election and increasing its powers, has run an assumption that, 'creating a Community legitimacy means creating an autonomous European power, or at least a Community

---

[17] Fitzmaurice, *op. cit.,* 1978, p. 139.

[18] Report of the working group on the problems of enlarging the powers of the European Parliament, EC Commission, Bulletin, Supplement 4/1972. The group appointed by the Commission with an advisory status consisted of 'experts' chosen from the nine States of the enlarged Community plus Norway.

[19] Pp. 53, 120–4.

power less dominated by the national capitals'.[20] The Commission itself has consistently supported a stronger Parliament from this point of view: 'the prospect of direct elections to the European Parliament holds out the hope that a fresh impetus will be given to the Community'.[21]

Perhaps, therefore, those who are sceptical about the Parliament from the point of view of democracy have some justification to suspect that the real aim might be simply to further European integration, or at least strengthen the Community along supranational lines. But there is a real problem for those who look to a reinforced European Parliament as a means of restoring supranational authority. While they would resist strongly any suggestion that they were not equally interested in the democratic effects, they are nevertheless begging a lot of questions when they suppose that greater parliamentary democracy at Community level will also mean greater political support for European integration or for a more dynamic Community. Indeed, it is not very clear what those objectives mean and that is why I shall devote some space to discussing them in Chapter III.

The various political forces in the directly elected Parliament will no doubt form their own view and draw their own conclusions. I have already indicated that the effects of direct elections could be mixed, even where the authority of the Parliament itself is concerned. But a stronger Parliament does not necessarily mean one that slavishly supports some official Community view of the general interest. Indeed, as I have also indicated, it is difficult, if not impossible, to identify any such official view to support or oppose. Would the Parliament therefore be expected to have its own view and make that official? That is to beg a number of questions in turn about the nature of parliamentary assemblies in general and about that of a directly elected European Parliament in particular. We need a clearer understanding of the role of parliaments in general and especially in the Member States of the Community and that will be the subject matter of Chapter IV.

A similar dilemma has been met in attempts to assess the performance of the European Parliament up to now. Is the Parliament intended to act essentially as a source of political will directed towards further integration, or as a forum where political differences about the Community's future can be ventilated? Or perhaps the two are compatible and indeed interdependent? Before going further into these questions, it is necessary to understand the role the Parliament has played up to now and especially in recent years as the prospect of direct election has come closer and as its demands for greater powers have increased. A good deal has already been written on the history of the Parliament and on its powers and organisation, so my account that follows in Chapter II will be concerned mainly with those characteristics that are likely to be significant for the institution's future.

---

[20] C. Sasse, Le Renforcement des pouvoirs du Parlement, in Institut d'Études Juridiques Européennes, *op. cit.*, p. 63.
[21] EC Commission, Eleventh General Report 1977, Brussels February 1978, para 1.

II The European Parliament Today: Present Role and Future Prospects.

Fundamental constraints on the Parliament's role

There is a crucial reason why the role of the European Parliament differs fundamentally from that of other parliaments we know. It is that the Community itself is unique, matching neither previous federations of independent nation states nor other methods of conducting international relations.

It is for this reason that the European Parliament cannot be compared to parliaments within the Member States, not as is more often supposed, because it lacks the status or power we commonly associate with a parliament. For one thing, as I shall consider at some length in Chapter IV, it is not possible to agree on a general definition of what a parliament is, even for the Community's Member States. Empirical evidence is simply not enough, beçause people have widely different ideas about what a parliament is or should be. We need, therefore, to assess what the European Parliament does, in terms of the Community's nature and objectives and of the Parliament's present status-and power and not only in terms of abstract definitions of the functions of parliaments.

Conversely, however, the very fact that the Community has the special powers it has, and that the European Parliament plays a role in their implementation, means that the Parliament cannot be compared to bodies like the Parliamentary Assembly of the Council of Europe or the Western European Union Assembly. The European Parliament has always had much greater significance than a mere international assembly, which is one reason no doubt why it has successfully claimed the title of 'Parliament', and also why many people have tried to deny it that title for fear of the special significance it implies. Indeed, one question about the European Parliament is why it has not made more use of its status and powers in order to make greater impact.

One answer is that we have to take account of certain fundamental limitations on the Parliament's role that direct elections or even changes in formal powers cannot in themselves alter. One of these limitations which is not to be found in parliaments elsewhere, is the fact that the Community's own powers are conferred by the treaties in relation only to specific measures and procedures for establishing a customs union and a common market and for achieving common

12

social and economic policies. The general aims of the treaties are, of course, much broader than that but they do not provide a central government in which the Parliament could play a part—even if only one of support or opposition. The absence of a constitutionally-established government at Community level makes the Parliament's role different from what it would be in a fully federal system of government. Another limitation is similar to that of many other parliaments where there is a constitutional separation of powers—the fact that its powers are fixed in relation to those of the other Community institutions.

These characteristics of the European Parliament in no sense mean that it is powerless. The question is, however, to what extent it is allowed to influence the development of the Community and in what ways and what ends its influence could be used. That is why the Parliament's history up to now is largely that of its efforts to find an effective role within certain fundamental constraints. Since the directly elected Parliament will find itself essentially in the same circumstances, assessing its future must depend to a great extent on understanding the result of those past efforts.

The Parliament as a representative assembly: composition, organisation and procedure

By far the most important aspect of the European Parliament as it already is, and one that is invariably under estimated, is its status as a representative assembly. However the Parliament may have been composed up to now, article 137 of the EEC Treaty describes it as consisting of 'representatives of the peoples of the States' and article 138 provides for its eventual popular election. The treaties thus provide an institution with far greater claims to political authority, however vague, than any other international assembly. Later articles in the same Section go on to give the Parliament vital autonomy in determining its own organisation and rules of procedure. Other articles in the EEC Treaty endow it with similar legal status to the other Institutions, enabling it among other things to bring actions before the Court of Justice on constitutional and other matters.[1] In these respects the Parliament enjoys an authority wanting in some State parliaments and not fully practised in any of them.

Composition

As to its composition, the Parliament's claims to be a representative assembly have of course been limited in practice because it has consisted, not of directly elected deputies but of national delegations appointed by the Member States' parliaments from among their own membership. For years it has been a major strategy of the Parliament to enhance its status by getting direct elections introduced in accordance with the treaties. It has been precisely the fear of the

---

[1] See pp. 129–31. Article 175 of the EEC Treaty enables the Parliament to bring an action 'should the Council or the Commission, in infringement of this Treaty, fail to act'. Such action has so far been no more than contemplated but is currently a possibility over the 1979 budget. Article 13 of the rules of the Court itself allows the Parliament to support the applications of parties to a particular case in which it can claim a direct interest.

governments of some Member States that the strategy would succeed that has delayed direct election until now. The likely consequence of direct elections will be treated more fully in the concluding chapter. To understand the Parliament's role, however, we should pause to consider just how and why the old method of selecting its members has been disadvantageous.

The old method has been defended on the grounds that, since power rests so much with the Member States themselves, the Parliament and the Community as a whole must gain from the participation of members of State parliaments. Indeed, there has always been considerable support for retaining the double mandate, at least partially, even with direct elections.[2] Students of the European Community have sometimes suggested that participation by State parliamentary delegates in the European Parliament may have served to shift the loyalties and interests of key political actors from a State to a European level.[3] From what studies have been made, however, it seems that most members of State delegations were either already more committed to European unity by the Community method than other members of State parliaments, or were sceptics who became better informed about Community issues but not converted.[4] There has on the other hand been a marked tendency for active members of European delegations to become detached from national political life under the pressure of serving a double mandate.[5] In the Coal and Steel Community in the 1950's, when the Assembly became a major battle ground for campaigns to create a European Political Community, leading politicians often went to Strasbourg and took the spotlight with them. In the EEC, however, as such expansive political issues receded in favour of more technical questions, the European Parliament became essentially an assembly of backbenchers. The Parliament has always included among its members some leading national party figures especially from the Benelux countries and Italy. On the whole, however, State delegations have been composed variously of unusually committed 'Europeans', backbench foreign affairs specialists or specialists in specific Community matters such as agriculture, and deputies typically sent on international delegations either to reward loyalty or to give relief to party colleagues. This has helped to give the Parliament the air of being a 'pro-European' pressure group rather than a genuine forum of political conflict and resolution.

The explanation is a largely inescapable one. Leaders of parliaments in the Member States are either members of the executive or are interested primarily in becoming so. Even in the Benelux countries and Italy, delegates to the European Parliament have become increasingly anxious about the adverse effects of European service on their careers. However, inveterate backbenchers by definition do

---

[2] See, for example, House of Lords Select Committee on the European Communities, Session 1977/78, 44th Report, HC 256-I.

[3] For example E. Haas, *The Uniting of Europe,* 2nd ed., (London, 1968).

[4] H. M. Kerr Jr., Changing attitudes through International Participation: The European Parliamentarians and Integration, in *International Affairs*, Vol. 27 No. 1.

[5] C. Sasse, et al., *Decision Making in the European Community*, New York and London, 1977, pp. 287–91, 324–6.

not usually carry the same weight in domestic politics as party leaders or would-be leaders. Certainly specialised backbench activity has far more influence in some national parliaments than in others. Indeed, there is evidence that the double mandate has sometimes enabled members to concert European and State parliamentary action on Community issues.[6] As the double mandate declines after direct elections, some substitute will have to be found for maintaining contact, communication and even co-operation between the two levels.[7] But the old method of selection cannot be justified only in terms of the value of concerted parliamentary influence for or against Community decisions.

The Parliament's composition (of 198 members since 1973) has not, on the other hand, entirely deprived it of credibility as a representative assembly. Smaller states have been over represented in terms of population. Direct election will not entirely change that and such a regional bias is not unusual even in the parliaments of unitary regimes. Indeed, a particular effort has been made in composing some State delegations to represent particular regional interests. Although majority parties in France and Italy were seriously over represented before 1970, while the Italian Communist Party was altogether excluded, the Parliament has come to include representatives of all the main political parties at national level, in spite of the wide variety of party systems among the Member States. The main social and economic interests affected by Community business have also been represented.[8]

Since we know that representation is an ambiguous concept and that in the experience of no Member State has parliamentary representation ever produced a perfect reflection of regional, party or socio-economic differences, is the old system that inadequate?[9] After all, in national elections we elect for the most part what are essentially nominees of established party machines, which are elector-ally effective mainly because they already have substantial strength in the national parliament. Membership in the European Parliament has depended on just such a process of national party selection and may well continue to do so to a large extent in the first direct election.[10]

Therefore, even under modern circumstances, where at least in theory legitimacy requires democratic representation, the Parliament has been able to claim greater authority in terms of popular representation than has usually been admitted. But there have been important shortcomings from the viewpoint both of democracy and of the Parliament's contribution to the development of the Community. The old method of selection has meant that the political balance in the Parliament shifts only in the most indirect and uncertain fashion in response to electoral or other political changes. This leads in turn to a lack of public

---

[6] *Ibid.* See also J. Fitzmaurice *The European Parliament*, (London, 1978), pp. 28–48, and House of Lords, *op. cit.*

[7] See pp. 132–3.

[8] Fitzmaurice, *op. cit.*, pp. 13–16, gives an excellent summary of the effects on composition of the old system. At present the Belgian Volksunie is the one major national party not represented.

[9] A. H. Birch, *Representation*, (London, 1971), pp. 51–60 and passim.

[10] See pp. 104–7.

involvement in the Parliament's business, or, to put it perhaps more significantly, a lack of public involvement in the business of the Community. While recognising that similar problems exist in national regimes, we should notice that other factors intensify them at Community level. Above all, there is not even a European electorate whose opinions can be tested by electoral means. The member of a State delegation has represented a constituency in relation to the Community only in the most tenuous sense, so that local communities cannot really identify with some direct parliamentary link to the Community. It can be doubted even within the Member States whether a parliamentary deputy's performance must affect his re-election. At a Community level it has been all the less likely. Finally, however, because the Parliament's members have had essentially to consider their performance at State level, the Parliament has lacked a sizeable group of members with the time, the physical capability, the interest or the passion to fight primarily on Community issues at a Community level.

In none of these respects should the results of the old method be under estimated or the prospects of direct elections be over estimated—especially in the attenuated form in which the first election has been arranged. If what matters, however, is the Parliament's right to act as the people's tribune, then direct elections, by increasing its credibility and facilitating its ability to function in practical ways, will certainly serve to make the Parliament more effective.

Organisation

At least as important as its direct election in giving practical effect to the Parliament's role as a tribune is the legal status it enjoys. In this respect it can claim institutional autonomy and power over such essential matters as its own organisation and procedure. Few, if any, national parliaments in Europe can exercise this in practice, and certainly not the British Parliament. Thus, according to the treaties, the Parliament meets as of right in annual session and it is up to the Parliament itself to decide when it shall sit and for what periods (in practice for twelve weekly 'part-sessions' a year).[11] In other words it does not rely on an executive body to convoke or dissolve it (as does the British Parliament) and the lengths of its sittings are not restricted by constitution (as are those of the French Assembly and Senate). In fact, the Parliament may even within limits decide where to hold its plenary as well as its committee meetings and it is restricted only by the Decision of the Heads of Governments of 8 April 1965 to treat Strasbourg as its official meeting place. In practice, the Parliament holds some plenary sessions in Luxembourg where its secretariat is based and its committees meet in Brussels and elsewhere.[12]

The Parliament elects its own governing Bureau, including its President and Vice-Presidents, which settles questions regarding the organisation of its secretariat (subject to the statutes governing employment and conditions of Com-

---

[11] EEC Treaty, article 139. The opening of a session takes place on the second Tuesday in March.

[12] Strasbourg is the seat fixed for the Parliament by the treaties, but by Rule 2/27 of its Rule of Procedures it may 'exceptionally', on a resolution of a majority of its members, decide to hold one or more plenary sittings elsewhere.

munity officials), the provision of services (such as the library, research and information departments and so on), the agenda of sittings and the allocation of business to committees (which meet even when the Parliament is not sitting).[13]

By a Resolution of the Council on 22 April 1970 the European Parliament gained sole responsibility for its own budget, provided its decisions on expenditure did not conflict with existing Community enactments or lead to a total Community budget that exceeded the maximum rate of increase fixed for that year. Indeed, the Parliament has substantial scope in providing facilities and services for its members, including office accommodation and repayment of expenses.[14] Although the government of the Member States claim the right to determine the level of salaries of directly elected members, the final decision legally rests with the Parliament itself. The Parliament will in any case determine the working conditions of its members, including such matters as indemnities and repayment of expenses. Its members are already protected in the same way as Community officials by the Protocol on Privileges and Immunities attached to the treaties, entitling them among other things to move freely across national boundaries when travelling to and from meetings of the Parliament or its committees.[15]

Procedure
Finally, subject to the treaties, the Parliament adopts and subsequently amends its own Rules of Procedure, which are implemented during sittings by its President and Vice-Presidents. In fact a number of procedures have been developed that enable the Parliament to play the role of tribune. The real power of a representative assembly always depends in practice, not only on its constitutional powers in relation to legislation, the budget and appointment of the executive but also on the political weight it is able to carry by holding public debates, questioning members of other institutions, holding committee investigations and issuing reports, and passing resolutions. In these ways assemblies exert influence on behalf of their electors by sheer moral pressure and by simply making themselves a general nuisance. The European Parliament is now well equipped for these purposes.[16]

In fact the Council now normally invites an Opinion from the Parliament on Commission proposals for Community legislation even where this is not actually required by the treaties. But the Parliament also reports, debates and expresses its views on its own initiative and on a wide range of matters, not only on formal

---

[13] EEC Treaty article 140.

[14] The Parliament's share of the Community budget amounted to approximately £45m. in 1977. The annual cost of the UK House of Commons is currently about £13m.

[15] EEC Treaty article 142.

[16] It is worth mentioning also that the Parliament on its own responsibility, not only publishes verbatim reports of its proceedings (published in the Community's Official Journal), but also publicises itself in various ways, especially through its active Press and Information Department, see V. Herman and J. Lodge, *The European Parliament and the European Community*, (London, 1978), pp. 120–41.

legislative proposals from the Commission. The Parliament regularly employs the following procedural means for raising matters on its own initiative:

Debates on motions for a resolution, which may be put down by any member (and are usually submitted to one of the Parliament's committees for report).

Debates, followed usually by the adoption of a resolution, on the report of a committee made on the latter's own initiative or at the request of the Parliament or one of its members.

Urgency debates, held with the Parliament's consent, at the request of the President or by at least ten members.

Consideration of petitions presented to the Parliament by any citizen of one of the Member States (though this usually takes place in committee).

Written Questions by any member to the Commission, Council or Foreign Ministers meeting in political co-operation, the Question and its answer being published in the Official Journal of the Communities.

Oral Questions without debate, which may also be put down by any member but must be selected for oral answer by the Parliament's 'enlarged' Bureau (see below).

Oral Questions with debate (a kind of interpellation procedure), which need to be put down by a committee, a political group, or five or more members, and may be terminated by a motion for a resolution to be voted on immediately.

Question Time which is held for not more than $1\frac{1}{2}$ hours on the second and third day of each sitting and during which any member may put questions so long as they have been declared admissible by the President.[17]

Questions constitute a formal power of the Parliament accorded to it by article 140 of the EEC Treaty. The use of Oral Questions has grown markedly since 1973 and the Parliament's rules of procedure governing their use have been greatly elaborated. Before the close of Question Time any political group of five or more members may request that a one hour debate be held immediately afterwards on an answer given on behalf of the Commission, the Council or the

---

[17] For example, during its sitting from 13–17 February 1978, the Parliament considered the following matters by procedures of this type: *Oral Questions with debate* on the regional effects of steel policy (raised by a group of Irish members), on financial aid to Greece, on the cancellation of a rail service to Strasbourg, on the road haulage tax in Austria (raised by a group of German members), on equal pay for men and women (raised by Socialist members), on the North-South dialogue, on international recognition of human rights, on energy policy, on a recent Court judgement affecting the implementation of the common agricultural policy (raised by the Parliament's committee on agriculture), on employment subsidies (raised by some UK Labour members), on the common market in fertilisers, on data-processing, and on negotiations with Cyprus; *debates on committee reports* on a Council resolution on the preparation of young people for work, on the date of direct elections, on the need for a single designation for the Community, and on the role of small and medium size undertakings in the Community (also an Oral Question with debate); numerous Oral Questions were also put during Question Time and were answered by the relevant Commissioners and by Danish ministers representing the Council. The time of the sitting was distributed as follows in terms of pages of the verbatim report (total: 289): 34 on internal procedural business, 132 on own-initiative proceedings, 123 on opinions on legislative proposals.

Conference of Foreign Ministers. According to the treaties the Commission is obliged to answer the Parliament's Questions but the Council, though not so obliged, normally also makes a ministerial representative available to answer the Parliament's Oral Questions. One week's notice has to be given to the Commission and five weeks to the Council for both kinds of Oral Questions (with or without debate). Written Questions (813 in 1976) have always been widely used, though mainly by a certain number of individual members, to raise particular matters with the Commission, and increasingly with the Council and the Conference of Foreign Ministers.

In general throughout the 1970's the Parliament has devoted an increasing proportion of its time to dealing with matters on its own initiative rather than at the invitation of the Commission or the Council in accordance with legislative or budgetary procedure, so that now normally nearly half of any normal sitting is spent in this way.[18] One explanation is the relative decline in the number of legislative proposals on major policy issues. Nevertheless, there has been a growing tendency for members of the Commission and increasingly of the Council too, to be willing to participate in the Parliament's proceedings, and even to make statements there on their own initiative. In addition, the Parliament's specialised committees keep in fairly regular touch with the Commission at official as well as Commissioner level, and are beginning to investigate matters, whether or not they are the subject of Commission proposals. There have been experiments with public hearings by committees.[19]

Naturally, to be influential by these means the Parliament depends on the resources of time and energy available to its members and on the political weight they can summon by concerted action. However, as with all parliaments the ability to act effectively on one's own initiative is a vital adjunct to wielding formal legislative, budgetary and other powers.

The Parliament's powers: advice and supervision

As for what can be regarded as the Parliament's formal powers of intervention, these are explicitly limited by the treaties to 'advisory and supervisory powers'. They derive essentially from two sets of treaty provisions. First, provisions for specific legislative measures on which the Parliament has to be consulted, of which there are eighteen in the EEC Treaty and eleven in the Euratom Treaty. Secondly, provisions making the Commission in effect collectively responsible to the Parliament, in particular article 144, by which the Parliament may force the Commission to resign by passing a motion of censure.[20]

The Parliament's history has been marked by its efforts to make these veritable powers of legislation and control. However, in recent years it has been in relation to its role in deciding the Community's annual budget that the Parliament has intervened most effectively. The Parliament's budgetary powers were signific-

---

[18] The proportions are different during those part sessions (chiefly in October and December) when the Parliament deals with the Community budget.

[19] See D. Sidjanski, *Auditions publiques dans la Communauté Européenne*, (Geneva 1976), pp. 39–81.

[20] The Commission is also obliged to reply to the Parliament's Questions (article 140.3) and to submit to it an annual report (article 143).

antly extended by the so-called Luxembourg Treaty of 1970 and by subsequent decisions but it is for the most part only in the last few years that they have begun to be fully exercised. As they are being now developed, they represent the most important formal opportunity for the Parliament in the immediate future, and I shall consider them later.[21]

The effectiveness of the Parliament's advisory power depends essentially on the attitude of the two main institutions in the process of making Community law: the Council and the Commission. It is not always obligatory to consult the Parliament and, even when it is, there is no obligation to accept the Parliament's views. It is in this respect above all that people have questioned whether the Parliament is really an institution worthy of its name.

On the other hand we know that parliaments in the Member States often exercise their legislative powers in little more than a formal sense, because important legislation is invariably prepared and introduced by the executive to be no more than debated, reviewed and ratified by parliament. Given that a fixed majority in most parliamentary assemblies in Europe is committed in practice between general elections to supporting an executive of its choice, even parliament's powers to amend and reject measures may be exercised only in special circumstances. There is a case for saying, therefore, that the power to be consulted and to state openly opinions on specific measures before they can become law, might be enough, if political influence can be exerted by other means. Often parliaments claim attention, not because of their formal powers of intervention but because they represent interests and opinions that the executive cannot afford to overlook.

It is not so much of a departure from normal parliamentary practice, therefore, that the European Parliament has no formal power of initiative in legislation. A more serious limitation is its lack of formal power to reject legislative proposals. But all the same it is unlikely that such a power could ever be exclusive to the Parliament, in view of the need to give a similar right to representatives of States' governments in the Council. A more realistic question is whether the Parliament's present powers could give it an effective means of amendment and of ultimate veto that could be used (as they are in national parliaments from time to time) in a positive way.

The Parliament and the Commission

In the first place it is up to the Commission whether the Parliament can block measures, or parts of measures, going to the Council for enactment. The relevant treaty provision here is article 149 of the EEC Treaty, which empowers the Commission to alter the legislative proposals it makes to the Council 'in particular where the Assembly has been consulted on that proposal', and limits the Council's power to reject such alterations (or 'amendments') by insisting that it can only do so unanimously. In practice these provisions mean that the Parliament could amend and even ultimately veto legislative measures on three

---

[21] See pp. 124–5.

conditions: that they were measures on which it must be consulted; that the Commission decided to withdraw and subsequently amend its original proposal to take account of the Opinion voted by the Parliament; and that at least one State's representative in the Council decided to support the Parliament's Opinion and so refused to reject the amendment or amendments concerned.

Much depends, therefore, on the Parliament's ability to get the Commission to take its views into account. Of course, the Commission is responsible to the Parliament, which has the ultimate sanction of passing a motion of censure. That sanction is limited in operation, however, because it would have what has been called a 'blunderbuss' effect. (Indeed, only four motions have ever been moved, only two of them taken to a vote, all in the last seven years). It would not only bring home to the Commission where its loyalties lie on any particular issue but actually reject its whole programme of measures. Moreover, the same Commission would continue in office until the Member States' governments appointed a new one. The fact is that the Commission's loyalties must also be to the governments of Member States, not only because they appoint it but because the consent of their representatives in the Council is required for any significant progress to be made. In practice the relative weight attached by the Commission to these different loyalties must be a matter of degree. Up to now there have rarely been major differences between the Commission and a majority of the Parliament's members on particular legislative proposals. But is is impossible to tell whether that is mainly because the Commission has actually taken the latter's views into account (if not by amending its proposals, then by consulting the Parliament before making any proposals and incorporating its main opinions), or because the Parliament has been obliged to accept that, if any progress is to be made at all, the Commission must be left a relatively free hand in conducting negotiations with the States' governments and their representatives in the Council.

Since opinion in the Parliament so far has been overwhelmingly committed to the broad aims of the Commission, it is not surprising that it has had little interest in blocking the latter's legislative proposals. Its amendments have been on the whole technical and superficial. The Commission has always gone out of its way to keep the Parliament informed of its proposals and of its general views, mainly by means of the Parliament's specialised committees, which regularly meet with Commissioners and their officials. Commissioners participate in plenary sittings when committee reports are being debated and resolutions containing amendments considered and passed. As direct election has become a reality, the Commission has in the last few years come to regard the Parliament's Opinions as having special weight. Since 1973 it has reported to most sittings on the way it has treated the Parliament's amendments up to date. An increasing majority have in fact been accepted.[22]

---

[22] In the years 1975 and 1976, 281 proposals were made by the Commission: 207 were accepted by the Parliament without amendment, 74 were amended by the Commission following the Parliament's Opinion, and in 52 proposals the Parliament's amendments were not accepted. On becoming President of the Commission, Mr. Roy Jenkins confirmed that the Commission would take a more positive view of the Parliament's amendments in view of direct elections. EC Commission, EC Bulletin 1/1977. Pt. 1/1/9.

Even if the Commission should decide to send to the Council only proposals that the Parliament's majority had explicitly and openly approved, however, there would still be major limitations on the Parliament's influence arising from the attitude of the Council.

The Parliament and the Council

In fact, the Council does now normally consult the Parliament before enacting measures, whether or not the treaty provisions oblige it to do so and even before making the increasing number of decisions that now effectively determine Community policy and its implementation without having the strict force of Community law. However, it is still possible for it to avoid involving the Parliament by choosing to base its action on some article of the treaties that does not require or imply that the Parliament should be consulted.[23]

A second and more important limitation arises from the refusal of the Council to consider proposals until they have been discussed first by the Committee of Permanent Representatives (COREPER), consisting of States' representatives at official level and charged with preparing the business of Council meetings.[24] Many matters are effectively decided in that Committee, and others get interminably held up there, or in lower level committees and working groups of State civil servants. Thus, not only are there usually quite enough sources of delay and obstruction without the Parliament needing to intervene but the Commission's proposals can get substantially amended well before the Parliament's own views (whether negative or not) can actually be taken into account.

The effects of this on the Commission's power of initiative and the Parliament's power of amendment have been made all the worse by the insistence of the States' governments on deciding matters by unanimity, even at the level of preparation by officials. One consequence is to make it more difficult than ever to get proposals beyond the stage of COREPER; in other words, there is often nothing even for the Parliament to obstruct or threaten to obstruct.[25] Another is that it becomes impossible for the Commission to build up coalitions to support a package of measures on the basis of majority voting. One strategy, in other words, might be for the Parliament's amending power to be used, with the support of one or more States' representatives, to threaten to block particular measures (say, an increase in agricultural prices) until others were passed in the form proposed by the Commission (say, an increase in aid to declining industrial areas, or protection for fishing stocks). Such strategies are not only perfectly compatible with the treaties but are actually necessary to co-ordinate different interests in any pluralistic system of government. But the States' governments in

---

[23] For example, in the recent case of proposals on fisheries policy, EP Debates No. 226 February 1978 pp. 121 ff.

[24] See the same example and also the proposal on trade co-operation with developing countries, EP Debates No. 224 December 1977 pp. 179–80.

[25] A typical example arose in the debate on a Commission proposal on coal stocks, where all speakers whatever their differences about the type of intervention required, devoted their time mainly to criticising the Council for inaction, EP Debates No. 220 September 1977, pp. 9–19.

the Community have become increasingly reluctant to break their rule of solidarity in face of Commission and Parliament for fear of allowing them greater influence.

In general, therefore, while we can see that the Parliament does have a role in legislation, we can also see the limitations of a power of amendment that cannot be backed by one of final approval. What is there to ensure that the views of a majority of the Parliament members are actually taken into account? We have seen that there is the Commission's ability to use article 149 (severely limited as that is in practice). It may also intervene on the Parliament's behalf during the Council's own deliberations and in those of COREPER. Since the Council's and COREPER's deliberations are held in private, there is no official means of knowing which governmental representatives are responsible for a particular decision, or even whether a decision is made in effect by the ministers themselves or by civil servants in COREPER. In any event the Council's decisions are final and it is not accountable to any other institution. It makes the final decision on whether or not to proceed with a particular measure and whether to enact it in one way or another. On general legislation the treaties provide no procedure for the Parliament to come back at the Council after the latter has decided: it has no final sanction either to make the Council act or to stop it from acting.

Nevertheless, the Parliament has developed its own procedures, in co-operation with the other Institutions, for following up what happens to its legislative amendments. We have already considered some of these in dealing above with the use of Questions. In fact, Oral Questions with debate have been increasingly used by members of the Parliament seeking to get explanations from the Commission and the Council as to why its views have not been taken into account, including explanations for failure to act on Commission proposals. Representatives of the Council, in the person of the minister for the subject concerned from the government currently holding the Presidency of the Council, are regularly appearing at plenary sittings to answer Questions on these lines. Of course, the answers are invariably unsatisfactory, being either evasive or helplessly sympathetic—implying that *that* minister has done his best to defend the Parliament's view, but cannot account for his colleagues.[26]

The holding of such 'dialogues' with the Commission or the Council have been greatly facilitated during the 1970's, as the governments have become increasingly anxious about the Community's poor public image, especially in the new Member States admitted in 1973, and as the Parliament's right to budgetary powers has been successfully asserted. In 1973 both the Commission and the Council announced practical measures to improve their relations with the Parliament, reinforcing the influence of the latter's procedures in the ways already noted here. The Commission's President now regularly makes a major address to the Parliament in February each year when the Commission's annual report is presented, and in it he is now expected not only to deal with the Commission's past record but also to present the broad lines of a programme for the future. The

---

[26] See, for example: EP Debates No. 220 September 1977, pp. 203–9; No. 223 November 1977 pp. 99–100; and No. 224 December 1977 pp. 179–80.

Commission takes the view that the Parliament should be consulted as a matter of course even where the treaties do not specifically provide for it and that its legislative proposals should be available to the Parliament as soon as they are submitted to the Council, without waiting for the latter formally to invite its Opinion.[27] For its part the Council has undertaken:

> not to deal, save in special cases, with any proposals from the Commission submitted to the Parliament for its Opinion, before it has received that Opinion provided that Opinions are given within reasonable time, which can in given cases be decided by common consent.[28]

The Parliament is now informed through its relevant committees of the progress of negotiations on external trade agreements and of the result of negotiations before agreements enter into force, as well as being consulted formally before agreements are ratified. The President-in-office of the nine foreign ministers, meeting in political co-operation, who co-ordinate Member States' foreign policies, also now reports to the Parliament annually and to its political committee quarterly.[29]

Since 1975, however, as part of the series of constitutional changes affecting the Community's budgetary procedures, the Parliament's means of influence have been significantly increased by the introduction of what is called the 'conciliation procedure'. This results from an agreement among the Institutions that, when legislative proposals have important financial consequences (in other words, 'money bills'), the Commission may indicate that a conciliation procedure should be applied for resolving differences between the Parliament and Council. The procedure takes place when the Parliament passes amendments by a substantial majority and when these are subsequently rejected by the Council. A special committee is formed of nine delegates chosen by the Parliament, the nine ministers representing their governments in the Council for the subject concerned and a representative of the Commission. A time limit of three months is set for reaching agreement and if there is no agreement in that time, the Council takes a final decision only after the Parliament has been allowed to present a second opinion (or in practice a revised set of amendments). The procedure has been adopted formally only once so far, when financial regulations to govern aspects of the budgetary procedure were proposed in 1977. The Council on this occasion rejected 36 out of the Parliament's 42 amendments to the Commission's original proposal and the conciliation committee having narrowed the essential disagreement down to five or six items finally resolved it to the Parliament's and the Council's satisfaction.[30] The procedure resembles a good deal procedures used in some federal systems (like that of West Germany) to resolve

---

[27] See Commission, *Practical measures to strengthen the powers of control of the European Parliament and to improve relations between the Parliament and the Commission*, Brussels 30 May 1973, COM (73) 999.

[28] Official Journal of the EC, Annex. No. 162, 1973; EP Debates No. 167 October 1973, pp. 69–70.

[29] See *Powers of the European Parliament*, London Information Office of the European Parliament, February 1978, pp. 29–31.

[30] See EP Debates, No. 224, December 1977, pp. 42–52.

24

differences between the popular chamber and that representing States' governments. However, it does not seem to oblige the Council to come to an agreement with the Parliament when the time limit is exhausted. Some members of the Parliament have maintained that conciliation should be renewed if necessary, after the Parliament has given a second opinion, until a final compromise is obtained. The procedure is now being invoked for the revision of the Regional Development Fund, and might be extended to aid to non-associated developing countries, the agricultural prices review, and the Community's power to raise loans. It has been argued that the Council should go one step further, since practically all legislative proposals have financial implications, and attempt to reconcile its views with those of the Parliament on all new measures. These and other proposals for strengthening the Parliament's legislative powers will be considered further in Chapter V.

The Parliament's budgetary powers

However, by far the most important breakthrough for the Parliament in its search for effective means of intervention has come with its acquisition of real budgetary powers. These powers have been obtained essentially as a result of two major developments in the Community budget itself. First, in 1970 after a prolonged struggle the Community finally acquired its 'own resources' for financing expenditure and subsequently, by stages, Community expenditure has largely ceased to be financed from specific contributions made by the States' governments. Giving the Community power to finance its own budget and to decide the amount and allocation of its own expenditure clearly has important economic implications, not least in promising to make Community expenditure more efficient. Such a step was not only envisaged by the treaties but virtually made inevitable when it was decided in 1962 to establish common financial means for implementing the common agricultural policy.

The second major development leading to changes in budgetary procedure has been the expansion of the Community budget into something far more than a means of accounting for administrative expenditure. Although it is still paltry in amount, if compared to public expenditure in the Member States, the Community's annual expenditure of about £8,000 million includes substantial intervention in agricultural markets, support for social, regional and industrial development and aid to overseas developing countries.[31] In other words, it is beginning to involve politically important decisions about the allocation of resources, apart from being in itself potentially a major instrument for influencing social and economic conditions.

Some State governments made it an essential condition of these developments that the European Parliament should be given enhanced powers of control, on the traditional principle of 'no taxation without representation'. In fact, in terms of a posteriori control the Parliament has now become the supreme budgetary authority that gives the final legal discharge allowing expenditure to be made

---

[31] D. Strasser, *The Finances of Europe*, (New York and London, 1977); D. Coombes, *The Power of the Purse in the European Communities*, (London, 1972).

from the budget each year, on the basis of a report of the Community's independent Court of Auditors. Indeed, the Parliament has decided to play an active part itself in checking on the legality and efficiency of previous expenditure by setting up, as a sub-committee of its committee on budgets, its own committee of control with the task of carrying out investigations both at Community and national level.[32]

Important as it may be, however, this sort of control is not the main part of budgetary decision making. What matters is how much the Parliament can determine: (a) the size of overall expenditure in relation to revenue, (b) the allocation of expenditure among different purposes, and (c) whether funds are actually used once voted. Its new powers still leave it with very limited influence in all these respects but they have meant that the Parliament's treatment of the budget has become the high point of its annual session, that its committee on budgets has gained increasing authority within the Parliament, and that the Parliament is coming to see the budget as its chief opportunity to determine Community policy.

As the new budgetary procedure is likely to play a major part in the directly elected Parliament, it is worth explaining how it has come to be applied during the past five years since the Luxembourg Treaty came into force. As with legislative proposals, the Parliament has no formal initiative (except where its own expenditure is concerned), and it is the Commission's responsibility to present the preliminary draft budget (based on estimates submitted by each Institution).

However, before the preliminary draft budget is presented (usually in June) the Commission now presents (in the early spring) a paper on budget strategy, which is debated in Parliament. It also fixes the required maximum rate of increase in expenditure allowed for the ensuing year's budget (on this see more below). The Council, on the basis of the Commission's preliminary draft, establishes the draft budget for the ensuing year. Normally the Council (consisting of finance ministers) starts by cutting expenditure proposed by the Commission 'across the board', that is, lopping off a certain percentage from each main item, with the exception of the estimated expenditure of market intervention in agriculture, which depends on later decisions on farm prices and cannot be predicted with any accuracy.

As has been widely commented, this is an extremely irrational and inefficient procedure of determining expenditure. The Council seems to pay hardly any attention to the questions of policy on which the budget is (or ought to be) based, or even to the question whether expenditure is allocated in the best and most efficient way to achieve its objectives. As the Commissioner responsible for budgets recently said:

---

[32] European Parliament, *The Case for a European Audit Office*, (Luxembourg, September 1973), and *The Budgetary Powers of the European Parliament*, (Luxembourg, October 1977), PE 49.730, pp. 21–24.

the Council has always approached the budget as an accounting exercise, the mechanical operation by which the funds are found for policies decided elsewhere.[33]

It is in this extremely unsatisfactory form that the Parliament receives the budget proposal, to which it may propose alterations (usually in September or October). Its ability to take a coherent, rational view is in turn limited, however, because its power of amendment applies fully only over those categories of expenditure that are considered as not flowing 'obligatorily' from previous Community decisions. Expenditure on agriculture, which accounts for 75 per cent of the whole budget is so considered.[34] On such items of expenditure the most the Parliament can do is to propose 'modifications' that the Council must then consider but is not obliged to accept. The voting procedures laid down give some chance that the Parliament could force reductions in this expenditure, if some States' representatives were willing to support it.[35] In fact, as many members of the Parliament complain bitterly, the Council does not accept significant changes in this 'obligatory' expenditure. Consequently what is left over for other expenditure tends to be severely limited by what the Council decides to claim for agricultural intervention (a sum which anyway will usually be increased by supplementary budgets in the ensuing financial year). On expenditure that is considered 'non-obligatory', however, the Council may only propose modifications to the Parliament's amendments, which the Parliament may (if it can secure a sufficient majority) in the end uphold, whatever the Council's opposition.

What the Parliament usually does is to replace most increases in spending proposed by the Commission but cut by the Council, though it is increasingly also making some expenditure proposals on its own initiative. Council and Parliament then proceed to settle their differences. In 1977, dealing with the 1978 budget, the Parliament and Council finally agreed to accept an overall increase of no more than £260 million (about three per cent of the total budget), but the Parliament considered this nevertheless as 'no small victory'.[36] In 1978, however, the failure of Council and Parliament to agree on the 1979 budget (mainly over increases in the regional fund) has provoked a constitutional crisis.

However, it is the Parliament that has the last word on the budget and in this way has the right to reject the budget as a whole. What is striking is the way that the Parliament, and in particular its committee on budgets, interpret this power as a responsibility to take a coherent view of Community expenditure, and to

---

[33] EP Debates, No. 220 September 1977, p.26.

[34] In summary, the 1978 budget was broken down as follows: Agriculture £5,979m.; Social policy £386m.; Regional policy £378m.; Energy £212m.; Development aid £350m.; Staff and administration £358m.; cost of revenue collection £449m.; other £150m.

[35] On this see further pp. 124–5.

[36] European Parliament Report No. 42 January 1978. The Parliament had originally proposed increases amounting to about £485m., mainly on the regional fund, social policy (for help to unemployed workers), nuclear fuel and hydro-carbon research, and increased development aid. One major controversy arose over the Parliament's right to increase expenditure on the regional fund, i.e. whether this was 'non-obligatory' expenditure. The heads of government themselves intervened to stop the Council accepting the Parliament's full amendments on this item and largely succeeded.

counter the 'incrementalist' approach of the Council, with an attempt to draw out and consider the policy implications of expenditure. The reports of the committee on budgets, and the plenary debates on the budget, increasingly express such a rational approach to expenditure decisions within the limitations imposed by the need especially on 'obligatory' expenditure to reach a compromise with the Council. They make a genuine attempt to treat the budget as a policy instrument, and criticise the other Institutions for failing to consider the implications of expenditure in terms of revenue, for failing to make real choices about allocating expenditure (especially in relation to agriculture), and for evading budgetary discipline, both by leaving certain forms of expenditure outside the budget and by including indeterminate commitments that depend on further legislative decisions by the Council (and threaten to result in later supplementary budgets). The Parliament has shown itself capable of enough discipline to achieve a comprehensive and consistent stance, especially in view of the rigid time limits imposed by the procedure. The co-ordinating role of its committee on budgets is especially important here.[37]

The Parliament was tempted both in 1977 and in 1978 to threaten to reject the budget, and there were important divisions within it that I shall mention later. The possibility of such a step undoubtedly influenced the Council in accepting the Parliament's amendments in 1977.[38] Although rejection of the budget would probably have a similar 'blunderbuss' effect to the passing of a motion of censure, its force as a sanction should not be under estimated. In practice, the ability to reach a compromise with the Council depends a good deal on the use of a 'collaboration procedure' so called to distinguish it from the similar conciliation procedure for legislative proposals and to stress that for the budget, Council and Parliament meet as equal partners. This procedure has been used since 1971 in an effort to reconcile by means of mutual concessions the Parliament's and the Council's amendments after the Council's second reading of the budget proposal. An additional meeting (of the finance ministers and nine delegates from the Parliament) is held in July before the Council adopts the Commission's draft budget. Like the conciliation procedure such meetings provide an excellent opportunity to enter into a dialogue, not just with a minister acting as President of the Council but with all the national finance ministers at once. However it has been criticised in relation to the budget for inhibiting the Parliament's attempts to take an independent and consistent view, and for glossing over differences within the Parliament itself.[39]

Indeed, it is time to consider some general limitations on the Parliament's budgetary powers that explain why its efforts to use them to determine Community policy are frustrated through no fault of its own.

---

[37] See for example EP Debates, No. 220 September 1977, pp. 53–63; No. 222 October 1977, pp. 3–36, 38–87; No. 224 December 1977, pp. 52–90, European Parliament, The Budgetary Powers of the European Parliament *op cit.*

[38] See EP Debates No. 220, pp. 81–83.

[39] See EP Debates No. 220, pp. 39–40, 54. See also pp. 122–3.

Above all, the decision to give the Community its own resources of finance did not give it a general power to raise new revenue, or even to run into deficit. The treaties still require that the budget revenue and expenditure must balance and although new measures have been taken to give the Community further powers to raise funds on the capital market, new independent sources of revenue could be obtained only by further amendment of the treaties. The only genuinely variable component of the existing sources, moreover, is the tiny proportion of receipts from value added taxation (presently about 0.70 per cent) that is assigned to the Community (up to one per cent may be assigned). Delays in implementing measures for establishing this as a common system of taxation have been an added restriction on its use as a source of Community revenue up to now. This limitation underlies a more direct constraint on the budgetary procedure as a whole, which is that 'non-obligatory' expenditure may only be increased within overall limits fixed each year by the Commission by what is known as the *'maximum rate'*. There has been considerable dispute about the meaning of the relevant provisions for they seem to make the Parliament's own power of amendment (for example, of increases in the regional or social funds) depend on the Council's decisions regarding 'obligatory' expenditure (that is, agriculture). The rate can be exceeded by agreement with the Council and the Commission, and this is what happened in 1977.[40] In 1978, however, when the Parliament's version of the budget exceeded the maximum rate, agreement was not reached, hence the crisis mentioned above.

Other general limitations arise from the rules governing Community expenditure. First, there is the distinction between 'obligatory' and 'non-obligatory' expenditure, which is itself extremely uncertain in application to new forms of expenditure. It has been hotly disputed, for example, in relation to the regional fund. The Council uses the distinction among other things to prevent the Parliament from imposing budgetary discipline on expenditure that will arise from legislative rather than budgetary decisions. Otherwise, it is implied, the Parliament would have power over legislative proposals through the back door. The Parliament argues that it needs to consider expenditure as a whole so that it can take a responsible and consistent view. The States' governments somewhat hypocritically, however, maintain that such a view is unlikely to come from a parliamentary assembly. At the same time, the distinction implies that the Parliament may not make new expenditure (even if sources of income were available) on measures for which legislative provision does not already exist, although the Council habitually tries to do this.

Another general feature of Community expenditure adds to the Parliament's frustrations in trying to treat the budget as a genuine policy instrument, and makes it difficult to ensure that expenditure voted is actually made. It is that expenditure from the various Community funds to support social and economic development usually goes to reimburse States' governments for their own expenditure on approved projects. Some governments, for various reasons, do

---

[40] For a fuller account see Strasser, *op. cit.*, pp. 122–4; Fitzmaurice, *op. cit.*, pp. 153–7; European Parliament, The Budgetary Powers of the European Parliament pp. 6–12.

not forward enough claims to the Community, or do not otherwise make full use of the funds available, and, as a result, the policy objectives have been frustrated. Thus the Parliament, or for that matter any Community Institution, cannot determine whether funds are allocated effectively. The size of the budget, therefore, in terms of funds voted in any one year is not an indication of how much money has actually been spent. This can be used by the Council as an argument against accepting increased allocations for funds that have been under subscribed in previous years.[41] The Parliament could seek to get round these limitations by setting conditions for future expenditure as part of its amendments to the budget. It might use this technique also as a means of retaliating against the practice of including token entries and indeterminate commitments in the budget, which depend on future legislative decisions. For example, the Parliament could insist that particular items of expenditure should be implemented only with Parliament's explicit approval, or for purposes clearly stated by Parliament in a budgetary amendment. All this goes to show how budgetary and legislative power will eventually have to be harmonised.

The need for internal discipline in the use of budgetary powers has already been mentioned. One aspect of the rules is particularly important in that respect: the need for a special majority to pass amendments to the budget or to reject it as a whole. The majority required is particularly demanding, since not only must three-fifths of the votes be cast in favour, but also a majority of the Parliament's total membership (which means at present at least 100 positive votes). When voting finally took place on the 1978 budget, the application of these rules clearly frustrated a number of members and worked strongly in favour of those seeking above all a compromise with the Council. As it is the Parliament devoted nearly a whole morning to the taking of votes on that occasion.[42] Clearly, the effectiveness with which the Parliament is to be able to use the powers it is now wresting must depend on how it functions as a political organisation.

The Parliament as a political organisation: political groups, committees, the role of opposition

It is in fact in its nature as a political organisation that the European Parliament differs most markedly from parliaments in the Member States (and above all from what we have come to regard as the British model of a parliament divided essentially between government and opposition supporters). One difference from British and Irish practice is expressed particularly in the way the internal hierarchy of the Parliament is organised, though the formal pattern is reasonably familiar in parliaments on the Continent.

Unlike the Speaker in the British parliament, who is strictly an impartial presiding officer and nothing more, the President of the European Parliament, though he also presides in an impartial manner, actually exercises functions of

[41] See for example: EP Debates, No. 224 December 1977 pp. 58–60; No. 222 October 1977 pp. 38–55 passim.

[42] EP Debates, No. 224, pp. 187–200. For a useful summary of the Parliament's budgetary powers, see *Powers of the European Parliament, op. cit.,* pp. 16–23. See also M. Shaw, *The European Parliament and the Community Budget* (London June, 1978).

political leadership for the Parliament as a whole and plays a crucial part in decisions about organisation and procedure which in Britain are the preserve of the government of the day. In performing these functions the President is assisted by twelve Vice-Presidents and together they form the Parliament's Bureau. The President is elected annually by the Parliament's members voting by secret ballot and by absolute majority. Conventionally, the same President is re-elected for a second term, but the practice of choosing the incumbent according to an agreed rota among political interests has now given way to that of contesting his election on political lines.[43] In fact, the main functions of the Bureau are exercised by the 'enlarged Bureau', which includes the chairmen of the political groups. The political groups, which also play a vital role in the election of the bureau itself, are the most important factor in the Parliament's organisation, and their influence is decisive in all significant aspects of the Parliament's life. Their role in this respect resembles of course that of political parties in the parliaments of the Member States. But their own internal cohesion, and their distinctiveness in terms of political principle and attitude, while they are greater in some groups than in others, are much less than in major political parties at State level.

Political groups
The Parliament's Rules of Procedure make provision for the formation and organisation of political groups and the latter elect their own bureaus and appoint secretariats paid out of the Parliament's funds. So important is it to belong to a group that most groups include elements held together but loosely and not only because of differing nationality. In 1977, although there were members from 49 different national parties, all but a handful belonged to one of the six political groups. Of these, however, only the Socialists (who now form the largest group but fall far short of an absolute majority) include members from every Member State, though the Liberals and Democrats lack members only from Ireland. Formerly the largest and still constituting in many ways the nearest to an 'establishment' party within the Community, the Christian Democrats nevertheless represent a 'political family' that is a major force only in two of the large States (West Germany and Italy). Similarly the Communists cannot draw on significant political support from outside France and Italy. The British Conservatives continue to be mainly a distinct national force, while forming, with the support of two Danish Conservatives, a European Conservative group. Finally, three other parties each peculiar to one State—including current parties of a government majority in the French Gaullists and the Irish Fianna Fail—make up the disparate European Progressive Democrats.[44]

---

[43] For details of the procedures see: European Parliament, Rules of Procedure, pp. 7–12, and Sir Barnett Cocks, *The European Parliament*, (London, 1973), pp. 86–93.

[44] In June 1977 the size of groups was as follows: Socialist 64; Christian Democratic 53; Liberal and Democratic 24; European Progressive Democrats 19; European Conservative 18; Communists and Allies 17; Non-attached 3. On the role of the political groups in general see: J. Fitzmaurice, *op. cit.*, pp. 15–16, 90–129, and *The Party Groups in the European Parliament*, (London, 1975); G. & P. Pridham, The Party Groups in the European Parliament, in S. Henig (ed.) *Political Parties in the European Community*, (London 1979), pp. 245–99.

It cannot be said, therefore, that anything resembling a European party system has emerged. I shall return in Chapter V to the likely effects of direct election and recent attempts to form Community wide political federations on an electoral basis. Meanwhile it is clear that an additional key difference between the European Parliament's political groups and most national parties is that the former lack any distinctive organisation for seeking support among, and maintaining contact with, an electorate.

Nevertheless, at least in matters of procedure and organisation, the political groups have usually acted cohesively, both internally and among themselves. As a result, although excessive time and trouble have been spent sometimes in settling misunderstandings and disagreements, procedure and organisation have been managed smoothly, more smoothly one suspects than if political divisions were as evident in the European Parliament as they are in State parliaments. As it is, divisions within the groups and those which cut across groups are more significant than those which divide the groups from each other. Partly, of course, and to some extent especially since enlargement, the real divisions are on lines of nationality. For example, the scepticism of most of the British Labour members has done much to undermine the cohesiveness of the Socialist group, normally regarded as the most united group in the past. Differences within the groups are by no means always settled before a particular matter is treated in plenary session. Indeed, although the differences are frequently based on other than national lines, the leaders of State delegations within each group play a significant part themselves in the Parliament's internal hierarchy especially as members of each group's own bureau.

Specialised Committees

However, one reason why political differences, following group lines or not, are not more evident is the role played by the Parliament's specialised committees.[45] Unless it is treated by the urgency procedure or follows an Oral Question, a debate in plenary sessions is always based on the report of one of these twelve committees, introduced by its rapporteur and including usually a motion for a resolution (containing, for example, amendments to legislative or budgetary proposals). The political groups themselves play a decisive role in the selection of the chairmen and rapporteurs of committees as well as in that of their members. However, the effect of consideration in committee is usually to produce a compromise, though minority views are meant to be contained in the report, which may be subject to amendment in plenary debate. The main political differences are usually settled in fact during the committee stage, which takes place in private and the post of rapporteur, who introduces the report in plenary debate and may intervene at any time, can be crucial for the way a matter is

---

[45] Currently: Political Affairs; Legal Affairs; Budgets (these three being the most important); Economic and Monetary Affairs; Agriculture; Social Affairs, Employment and Education; Regional Policy, Regional Planning and Transport; Environment, Public Health and Consumer Protection; Energy and Research; External Economic Relations; Development and Co-operation; Rules of procedure and petitions. There are usually thirty-five members on each committee.

treated by the Parliament. It is a post that can be hotly contested among the groups. The chairman of a committee, however, has a more important continuing influence over its general attitude and 'philosophy', and these are more significant factors in determining the actual treatment of particular issues than the views of the political groups themselves. He is, among other things, able to influence the selection of topics for consideration, the timing by which they are considered, and generally the weight given to views opposed to those of the rapporteur himself.

The predominant role of committees, above all in legislative matters, is said to be responsible for the stilted and boring nature of the Parliament's plenary debates. However, the general air of tedium, and even of unreality, in which so much of the Parliament's public proceedings take place does not differ that much from what happens in many state parliaments when specialised legislation is being dealt with. It is not in itself a reason for arguing that the Parliament should devote less time to the literal business of examining particular legislative measures, or for supposing that such business is not potentially of political importance.[46]

Nor does it mean that the Parliament should, or could, dispense with the role its committees now perform. Committees are an essential means of providing continuity between sittings and specialisation among members and of overcoming various problems intrinsic to an international assembly. They are also indispensable, and are seen as such in most national parliaments in the Community, for an assembly that intends to participate in the taking of legislative and other decisions but whose numerous membership breaks up into many different political tendencies and loyalties, and one that is not prepared to leave either the principles or the details to the executive. That the Parliament's proceedings have so little appeal is undoubtedly explained most by the fact that it is ministers in the Council and not backbench MPs in the Parliament, whose support is required for getting measures enacted.

The role of opposition
In fact, important differences are extremely rare, and it has often been remarked that the Parliament does not contain a genuine opposition.[47] The conflict that runs below the surface throughout its work is essentially between the Parliament itself and the Council or the State governments that the latter represents. As I have described it elsewhere,[48] the Parliament is forced into the role of acting as an 'institution of opposition', and it is striking to what extent the different political groups in the end usually take up similar positions. Even the Gaullists, the Communists and certain British and Danish Socialists who might have been

---

[46] The Parliament's rules of procedure now allow for the lengthy procedure of committee reports to be evaded for non-controversial matters, see *Powers of the European Parliament, op. cit.,* pp. 14–15. For an excellent account of the role of the committees, see Fitzmaurice, 1978, *op. cit.,* pp. 17–24.
[47] Gerda Zellentin, The form and function of opposition in the European Communities, *Government & Opposition*, Vol. 2 No. 3: Fitzmaurice, 1975, *op. cit.,* pp. 196–7; Sasse, *op. cit.,* pp. 285–305.
[48] In Sasse, *op. cit.,* p. 337.

expected to form an 'anti-establishment' bloc in Community terms, have not sustained a clear opposition to the majority view for any period of time or over the same set of issues. Votes are rarely necessary in plenary sittings (though they are common in committees) and have become normal only when the Parliament exercises its new budgetary powers.

In this respect, and following earlier occasions when the Parliament was campaigning over what those powers should be, a significant division has emerged between what for want of better terminology can be called 'maximalists' and 'minimalists': the former seeking a harder confrontation with the Council and the latter stressing the Parliament's conventional attitude of 'not rocking the boat'. The division does not follow group or national lines.[49] It has been particularly blurred in budgetary proceedings by another division: that between supporters and opponents of the present common agricultural policy. There are clearly members from different groups and States who would like to wield budgetary powers with less regard for the continuity of Community policy making, if it were not for their support of the present nature and level of agricultural spending. When it comes to the crunch there has not been sufficiently disciplined support for doing other than following the Commission's lead and so avoiding a real confrontation with the Council.[50] The proceedings on the 1979 budget, however, have turned out to be an exception and may indicate a change of attitude with the prospect of direct election.

On the whole the Parliament seems to have been dominated by a kind of 'establishment' consisting often of the same long serving members, which fills most of its positions in the four top stages of its internal hierarchy as described here. The leadership thus offered has had the same consistent theme: united commitment to the broad aims of the treaties and usually also to the Commission's general strategy for pursuing them. Political and other differences have been seen as a potential threat and there has been a tendency to push party, national and other disputes below the surface. The major causes of this type of leadership have been dealt with in this chapter: the absence of a Community central government to oppose (the Commission falling far short of such a role); the vast superiority of the Council's powers compared to those of the Parliament; the lack of a real party system at Community level; the demand for discipline made by special majorities (as in budgetary procedure and passing a motion of censure) and by the conciliation and collaboration procedures.

However, it is as much as anything an establishment by default, since by no means all the Parliament's members have seen their role consistently as active or interesting. Absenteeism has often been a problem for procedure and organisation. There have been various special reasons for this absenteeism other than indifference, ranging from crucial votes in a national parliament to inclement

---

[49] See in particular EP Debates No. 224, pp. 187 ff. An example of the 'minimalist' position is Mr. Shaw's remark (British Conservative) that: 'it would be absolute folly to try to get everything just to show our muscle or for whatever reason it may be'. Cf. the attitudes considered in Sasse, *op. cit.*, pp. 300–2.

[50] See Mr. Spinelli's remarks, EP Debates No 224, p. 27. See also the Parliament's inability to summon a sufficient majority, EP Debates No. 223 November 1977, pp. 210–4.

weather and the hospitality of the mayor of Strasbourg.[51] The particular problem of low attendance (which is impossible to assess with any accuracy) has clearly arisen chiefly from the way the Parliament is composed, its shortage of formal powers, and the absence of sufficient authority at a Community level worth supporting or opposing. Up to now the Parliament's leaders have devoted much of their efforts to trying to get these circumstances altered and have probably been supported in that by most other members. What has really been lacking is a sufficiently clear and agreed idea of what the institution's true role should be.

An institution in search of a role
In Chapter I, I expressed the view that introducing direct elections not only falls far short of solving the Parliament's—or for that matter the Community's—main problems, but actually increases the urgency of settling the many doubts surrounding the future of the Parliament—and that of the Community. In this chapter I have suggested that the changes in composition made by direct election, in so far as they are predictable at all, will add to the Parliament's effectiveness mainly in practical ways—by giving it just over twice as many members, enabling them to offer full time service, providing much greater continuity in membership, and so on. More than this, all we can say at this stage is that the Parliament will obviously gain in moral authority, in 'democratic legitimacy' as it is called.

I shall consider the likely effects of direct elections more fully in Chapter V. Most of this chapter has dealt with the existing potential and the fundamental limitations of the Parliament's role under the Community system. One conclusion is that its independent status, its formal powers of intervention in Community law and policy making and those of control, and its means of political organisation already enable the Parliament to be a force to be reckoned with. In Chapter V, I shall return to the question of formal powers and to that of internal organisation and I shall discuss there how these aspects might be further developed within the present structure of the Community.

What we have seen in this chapter, however, is the way the Parliament is subject to constraints arising from the very nature of the Community and its decision making process. While it has acquired considerable opportunity to ventilate and dispute policies and actions of the Community, its proceedings and their outcome invariably lack practical impact simply because the Community itself has been unable in practice to deal effectively with many real problems. Much as it might goad or censure the Commission, the latter is usually unable to do more than to answer with humility and to plead impotence, which are precisely the sentiments which the speeches of its representatives normally express before the Parliament. Even if the Parliament—through the mediation of the Commission or by its own direct intervention—were able to fashion legislative and other proposals to its own requirements, Community law and policy making would still in the end depend essentially on the attitudes and behaviour of the governments of the Member Sates. The Parliament has found ways of getting

---

[51] For example, EP Debates No. 220, p. 216; No. 223 November 1977, p. 63; ibid. pp. 101–2.

on equal terms with the Council in certain respects—above all in budgetary matters, where it is even acquiring means of forcing the Council to accept its own views on particular issues. However, given the present constitutional framework, there are clearly limits to how far this relationship can go.

Two general conclusions follow. First, the Parliament's role can be understood only in relation to that of the other Community Institutions; in particular, within the present structure it cannot do much about its own power of intervention unless it takes account of that of the Commission, and however it tries to intervene it has to recognise the power of the States' governments. Secondly, it is impossible for the Parliament to find an effective role without considering the wider constitutional issues affecting the distribution of power between the Community and its Member States.

The directly elected Parliament, therefore, cannot avoid taking a view about the future of the European Community. I have already suggested in Chapter I that its choice of strategies faces it with a dilemma. It is expected to see itself as a forum for the expression of political differences, and that is an obvious enough role for a representative assembly—a role that it has been criticised with some justification for failing to play adequately in the past. But, as Dean Vedel has crisply put it:

> The question which must be discussed more fully—and which cannot be answered by slogans—is whether the development of the parliamentary institution, which undeniably constitutes a step forward for democracy, would also be a step forward towards integration.[52]

One problem for a European Parliament playing the role of democratic tribune will be to locate an authority against which its claims and grievances can be suitably made. As another astute observer of the Community's institutional development has put it: 'What is lacking in Europe is not a parliament but a government'.[53] Another problem, implied by that, and one that has sometimes tormented the Parliament in the past, will be deciding what limits should be placed on democratic responsiveness in the interests of building an acceptable Community.

Indeed, the Parliament is also expected to act as a source of renewed political will enabling the Community to overcome the spirit of doubt and disillusion that, in spite of expressions of grand design, has increasingly come to lead it into impasse and inertia. It is significant that the one major study of the Parliament's future role to issue from the Community itself (the report of the Vedel Group to whose work we shall return in later chapters) stressed above all the need to restore the institutional means of defending a common, European interest against the special, national interests represented by the Council and its ancillary organs. Can one be at all sure, however, that such a utilitarian approach will be welcomed by a directly elected representative assembly, or that it is truly compatible with such a body's democratic responsibility? If the Community lacks above

---

[52] European Parliament, *European Integration and the Future of Parliaments in Europe*, (Luxembourg October 1975), p. 239.
[53] E. Bubba, *La Mission du Parlement Europeen*, (Brussels, 1970), p. 94.

all effective means of centralised initiative and co-ordination, and if it must either proceed by further integration or else disintegrate, what realistic use can the future Parliament make of its democratic authority and of its present and future powers? What will be the point of obstruction and delay, of criticism and checks, if the alternative to action is chaos?

Clearly, before the choice of strategies, and their consequences in terms of powers and organisation, can be further considered we need more light on two subjects: the political needs of the Community itself, and the nature and purposes of parliamentary institutions.

III The future of the European Community: The need for political institutions

A positive view of the Community

The European Parliament's future role makes sense only in relation to a view of the future of the European Community. In this chapter, therefore, I shall go more deeply into the political implications of the Community's future development. The argument will be that any positive view of the Community's future must recognise a need for important changes in political institutions.

For all sorts of historical reasons, which have been widely treated elsewhere and do not need to be repeated now, the establishment of the Community was not accompanied by a constitutional settlement comparable to the settlements when federations were created out of independent sovereign States in the past. Nor has the Community yet led to a full settlement enabling the Member States to establish a new, central government common to themselves. It has not even raised the question of what sort of constitutional settlement—confederal, federal, unitary or otherwise—would be desirable. That question is hazy enough and students of law and politics are almost as disunited and perplexed about it as practical politicians, even with regard to existing and past systems of government let alone a hypothetical Community system.

The very idea that the Community should involve a full constitutional settlement has become increasingly hypothetical as opposition has grown to the supranationalism in the founding treaties. Thus the supranational elements in the Community have been increasingly seen as a threat to the sovereignty of the Member States considered by many to be the only effective and legitimate basis of government. Such an attitude is not entirely negative. It often accepts in general terms the broad principles and aims of the treaties and sometimes proposes its own vision of the Community's future.

General de Gaulle, above all, was often bitterly and radically critical of the Community and its methods from such a point of view but Gaullism claimed to have positive aims: to dispel dangerous illusions based on the 'chimera' of supranational authority; to counter a technocratic Europe confined to 'la froide économie'; to avoid buying unity at the cost of independence from the world, 'superpowers'; and to keep the doors open for unity including other nations of Europe to the south and east.[1]

Whether Gaullism was sincere in expressing these aims, or was not rather some neo-Hegelian exaltation of the nation state, we cannot deny that suspicion of supranationalism has continued since de Gaulle to influence both the practice and the theory of Community politics. In practice the tenacity of nationalism has been manifested in various ways in the organisation of the Community: the rule of unanimity adopted in the Council; the prevalent role of representatives of State governments in decision making; the relative decline of the Commission; the growing intervention of heads of governments; the feebleness of the established institutional machinery when trying to move from sectoral aspects to a global view (as in general economic or foreign policy); and the reliance on inter-governmental procedures where such wider questions have been treated in a co-operative manner. A typical response from someone with practical experience of the Community, favourable to its general principles and aims, is that of Ralf Dahrendorf, who has suggested that the inter-governmental methods adopted by the Community for extending its scope into foreign policy since 1969 (known as the 'Davignon formula') offer a far more realistic way of approaching integration in future than 'the supranational fiction' on which the Community initially based models of its future development.[2]

The new pragmatism that has consequently become so fashionable in the Community was reinforced by the accession of new Member States in 1973. The official policies of both major political parties in Britain do not exclude some form of federation in the long term but they have continued to stress as a condition of British membership that further constitutional issues will be left open unless and until Britain is ready to consider them.[3] Since their accession British and Danish governments have regarded as fundamental the right to veto proposals affecting their vital national interests. They have accepted direct elections to the European Parliament only with undisguised reluctance and on the understanding that no commitment to alter the existing balance of the Community Institutions is implied.

This pragmatism differs from Gaullism in its desire to eschew doctrinaire attitudes but it closely resembles Gaullism in action. It is profoundly sceptical of supranational methods, deeply attached to the sovereign nation state which it sees as the ideal form of government, and it is fearful of federalism as threatening to create a 'super-state'. At the same time it professes a genuine desire to seek co-operation within the Community framework so long and so far as it is in the State's interests to do so. Indeed, it has not prevented the enlarged Community

---

[1] F. R. Willis, *France, Germany and the New Europe*, 2nd ed., (London, 1968), pp. 292 ff. For a recent statement of Gaullist doctrine on Europe, see J. M. Benoist, *Pavane pour une Europe défunte*, (Paris, 1976).

[2] R. Dahrendorf, A New Goal for Europe in M. Hodges (ed.), *European Integration*, (London, 1972), pp. 74–78. See also S. Hoffman, Obstinate or obsolete, the fate of the nation state and the case of Western Europe, in *Daedalus*, No. 95, Summer 1966, pp. 862–915.

[3] See Roy Pryce, *The Politics of the European Community*, (London, 1973), pp. 165–60.

from substantially extending its sphere of interest beyond the subject matter of the founding treaties, or from setting highly ambitious new objectives, in particular that of 'transforming . . . the whole complex of the relations of member states into a European union' by 1980 and on the basis of the present treaties.[4]

The original Member States' decision to accept the application of the new members was really taken in 1969 along with the decision to complete the establishment of the Common Market. In spite of the difficulties implied by that enlargement, it did provoke a new dynamism in the Community. The Community's aims were subsequently extended by the Member States beyond the Common Market to include: measures to create an economic union (a part of which had already emerged mainly in the shape of the common agricultural policy and procedures of economic and monetary co-operation); regular consultation and co-operation in foreign policy; measures to protect and promote the welfare of the individual citizen beyond the economic sphere; and steps to strengthen democratic institutions (as in the introduction of direct elections to the European Parliament).[5] It was undoubtedly necessary to take a more realistic view of national sovereignty for this wider perspective to be accepted by the Member States' governments.

On the other hand the pragmatic approach that now prevails has a critical weakness. In spite of its healthy scepticism, it has little of substance to say about how political institutions need to be adjusted to take account of the growing economic and political interdependence of the Member States, the wider context of the Community's present problems, or the other consequences of establishing the Common Market. It has helped to show up some deficiencies of the Community but it falls back too easily on inter-governmental procedures, betraying a naive optimism of its own about the viability of existing forms of political authority.

A positive view of the Community's future should be no less critical but it should be far more constructive. It need not start by assuming that the Community is or ought to be a new political system but it should be willing to countenance forms of political authority beyond the existing nation states. It should recognise that, while the Community is *sui generis*, nevertheless something might be learned from the experience of existing or past systems of government. In other words, a positive view should be empirical, in the sense of trying to find practical solutions to problems defined by analysis—not pragmatic, in the sense of considering only solutions that appeal to a dominant interest or a prevailing view of events. I shall try in this chapter to suggest what such a positive view means for the future of the Community in terms of its political institutions.

The political needs of the Community
The Community's need for political institutions has been distorted by two

---

[4] Point 16 of the Final Communiqué, in EC Commission, Bulletin 10–1972, Part 1, Ch. 1.

[5] See, for example, EC Commission, Report on European Union; EC Bulletin, Supp. 5–1975, pp. 9–10; EC Commission, European Union, Report by Mr Leo Tindemans, EC Bulletin, Supp. 1–1976, Ch. I and Ch. II.

particular misconceptions about its political consequences. First, there is an idea that the Community's aims demand a cumulative transfer of powers of government from a national to a supranational level. Related to this, secondly, is an idea that the Community's effectiveness should be measured in terms of the weight of its own powers compared to those of the Member States.

As a reaction against those ideas there has been a tendency, influenced by the new pragmatism in the Community, to fall back on what seems to be firmer ground. Sometimes the main reaction is to seek the hard ground of national sovereignty by treating the Community as no more than a variation on previous forms of international relations between States. Sometimes it is to seek security in the generality of abstract concepts by considering the Community as if it were no more than a decision or policy making process. This is not the place to analyse the weaknesses of either of these recent, largely academic approaches but I hope to show that a different view of the Community's political needs is still possible, while nevertheless exorcising the idea that the Community's principles and aims somehow imply indefinite integration or a balance of governmental powers favouring the centre.[6]

The first step of exorcism must be to lay the ghost of the federalist 'super-state'. Not only has the Community never espoused such an aim but it has nothing to do with genuine federalism. For one thing a federalist would hardly evaluate the performance of the Community on the basis of a continuum:

... from a situation in which individual governments make all fundamental policy choices by means of a purely internal process of decision making ... to a terminal situation where all these choices are subject to joint decision in the European system ...[7]

Federalism is not an idea that the power of central government should be increased, or even that integration should be sought as an end in itself. It is rather a general model for the proper allocation of power between different levels of government. It seeks above all to set limits to the power of government. It may be criticised as indecisive, and even illusory, by those who cling to the idea of indivisible sovereignty; and it may be limited by its concern with the methods, rather than the substance, of government.[8] It is, however, politically hard headed enough to question the reasons for shifting political authority from one level of government to another. It is sufficiently concerned with constitutional issues to seek to set standards, in addition to 'unity' or 'integration', for the way in which government is exercised.[9]

---

[6] For a recent discussion see H. Wallace, W. Wallace and C. Webb, *Policy-making in the European Community*, (London, 1977), pp. 1–68. For treatment of the Community's development essentially as international relations, see mainly Hoffman, *op. cit.,* and D. B. Calleo, *Europe's Future,* (London, 1967). For the 'cumulative' and 'absolute' approach see mainly L. Lindberg and S. Scheingold, *Europe's Would-be-Polity*, (Englewood Cliffs, N. J., 1970).

[7] Lindberg and Scheingold, *op. cit.,* p. 68.

[8] See, for example, F. H. Hinsley, *Sovereignty*, (London, 1966), pp. 210–12, 235–6.

[9] See, for example, C. J. Freidrich, *Constitutional Government and Democracy*, 4th ed., (Waltham, Mass. 1968), pp. 188–95; G. Sawer, *Modern Federalism*, (London, 1969), pp. 183 ff; K. C. Wheare, *What Federal Government Is*, in P. Ransome (ed.), *Studies in Federal Planning*, (London, 1943), pp. 17–38; W. I. Jennings, *A Federation for Western Europe*, (London, 1940).

Here is at least one point of view, therefore, that gives the Community political significance without believing in integration or the transfer of powers as an overriding goal. Indeed, federalists can be just as anxious as anyone else about the consequences for the existing political order of European unification. If, for example, the aim were to create a European 'super-state' out of the Community, then genuine federalists ought to be among the first to be opposed. At present their main concern should be that the co-operative exercise of power by existing nation states in the Community is tending to evade constitutional checks and balances. But even so federalists are not the only people to be worried about the tendency for political power to be concentrated outside and across existing boundaries of legitimate government; and federalism may not be the only positive answer.

Indeed, the European Community was not founded on federalist principles, though some federalist thinking was influential in its conception and has continued to play an important part in its evolution. The Community's design does nevertheless seek to deal with the sort of political problems that are of concern to those like federalists who wish to contain political power in an established order. It does so in an original way distinguishing it both from other international organisations and from previous attempts to federate independent states. In this respect it has features that are at least as important for the study and practice of politics as the fact that it was born partly of a grand political design for Europe.

The Constitutional Framework of the Community

First, the Community goes far beyond other international organisations in the extent to which it seeks to embody agreements among its participating States in a system of law. In fact the relevant features of the Community's legal system have been clearly articulated elsewhere[10] but for the sake of understanding its political consequences they cannot be emphasised enough:

(a) Community law is independent of the Member States in the sense that it can be of direct incidence and may not require further enactment by Member States' public authorities to be fully binding on both public and private bodies and individuals.

(b) It takes precedence over the law of the Member States in the sense that the Court of Justice established by the treaties is the final authority in interpreting it; the role of the Court in developing the Community's legal framework is a political aspect of major significance.

(c) Community law is also generative, consisting not only of binding provisions of the treaties but also of secondary legislation which the Community's independent Institutions are empowered to enact, and of 'unwritten' law produced by decisions of the Court of Justice.[11]

---

[10] Lord Mackenzie-Stuart, *The European Communities and the Rule of Law*, (London, 1977); Legal and constitutional implications uf UK membership of the European Communities, HMSO, Cmnd. 3301, (London 1967); EC Commission, Opinion of the applications for membership received from the UK, Denmark, Ireland and Norway. (Brussels Sept. 1967).

[11] See J. D. B. Mitchell, The Rationality of the European Court of Justice, in *The Three Banks Review*, June, 1975, No. 106, pp. 62–84.

These characteristics of the Community are of profound consequence for the existing political order. They both limit the competence of political authorities within the participating States and create a measure of political authority in the Community's own Institutions. Above all, they mean that henceforth the State governments can be held responsible for acts covered by existing Community law only by procedures provided within the Community's own legal system. In practice therefore channels of influence and control leading solely to the State governments (and parliaments) lose some of their significance. Those individuals and organisations wishing to exert political influence have to some extent to redirect their attention to the Community Institutions.

The Community's legal system does, moreover, provide flexibility for responding to newly perceived and evolving needs. It embodies a fundamental principle that the distribution of power indicated by such needs should be decided and maintained by a due process involving formal and attributable acts. It even implies that the due process formerly entrenched within a State should not simply be abandoned along with the powers transferred to the Community, but ought to be re-established in the Community. How adequately a due process is so re-established is of course another question and this has proved to be a major political problem of the Community's development.

Secondly, the treaties leave the States with substantial, entrenched rights. The treaties (as the constitutional foundation of the Community) are the States' creatures, which can be amended only with States' unanimous approval. The States participate directly through their governments' representatives in the Council, which is the Community institution with by far the greatest power in making new Community law and policy. Indeed, for some critical objectives of the Community, in particular those concerning general economic policy, the treaties provide for procedures for co-operation and co-ordination among the States' governments rather than direct Community legislation. It does not make much sense, therefore, to try to measure the powers of the Community as if they were in an inverse relationship to the powers of its participating States. Nor can it really be criticised for under estimating the importance of national sovereignty.

There can be little doubt that, in providing for such a limited transfer of authority from the States, the framers of the treaties were facing up to political realities. Prevailing ideas of national sovereignty could not at the time be challenged any further and there was actually no consensus for doing more than creating a structure with flexibility for the future. The political realities seem in some essential respects to be even more constraining now. Certain conclusions can be firmly established, however, regarding the role of the States in the Community's future development.

In the first place, it is difficult to see how any major alteration in the powers and functions of the Community could be anything other than gradual. Indeed, no major constitutional rearrangement (even, for example, the foundation of the United States of America) has ever taken place without years of trial and error. Secondly, at no conceivable stage and on no reasonable grounds is it likely to be necessary to transfer the bulk of public administration within the States to a

43

d

Community level. A reverse trend might be more feasible, tilting the existing balance in favour of regions within the existing States. Even co-ordination of economic, social and other domestic policies and their effective defence and promotion overseas, do not necessarily require that all, or even much, law making and administration have to be centralised, whether at a State or a European level. Finally, in the Community as it is now and is likely to remain without a new, major constitutional act replacing or extending the existing treaties, it is the Member States that are sovereign. Only they can legitimately determine both the pace and the scope of any further transfer of powers and functions to the Community.

The third feature of the Community's design that is of special political significance is the recognition, however qualified, of the need for direct political representation at a Community level. We have seen how qualified this recognition is, both in theory and in practice, given the very limited powers of the European Parliament and given that its direct election has been so long delayed. However, in providing for a directly elected parliamentary assembly at all, the treaties acknowledge that the Community will call forth political opinions and interests that need their own means of expression alongside, but separate from, the Member States' governments. The independent policy making role of the Commission can also be seen as implying that the Community should develop its own procedures of political consultation and channels of influence, which can by-pass the States' governments. Indeed, the Commission's relations with interest groups organised at a European level have been of vital importance both in forming and in implementing the more integrated 'common policies', such as agriculture and external trade relations.[12]

Unfinished and partial as the Community's constitutional arrangements are, therefore, they do challenge the existing order even though they do not by themselves create a new body politic, or a federation. If we now turn to consider what the material attributes of the Community imply for politics, in particular its economic aims and achievements, the role of political institutions becomes even more clearly central to discussing future developments.

Consequences of economic integration
For two extremely important general reasons, the substance of the Community is irrevocably political as well as economic; in fact it is political partly because it is based on vital economic aims and principles.

The first reason, put at its most simple, is that in the modern, post-industrial state, economics cannot be extricated from questions of public policy or political principle. It is not necessary to rehearse here the explanations of why economic policy is nowadays central to all aspects of government, including the conduct of foreign affairs. Thus it is wrong to suppose, because the substance of the Com-

---

[12] On the role of interest groups, see Lindberg and Scheingold, *op. cit.*, pp. 141–82; R. Pryce, *op. cit.*, pp. 87–91, 179–81; D. Coombes, *Politics and Bureaucracy in the European Community*, (London, 1970), pp. 166–217; D. Sidjanski and J. Meynaud, *L'Europe des affaires: role et structure des groupes*, (Paris, 1967).

munity treaties is predominantly economic, that the Community would have to undergo a qualitative change before gaining political significance.

It is necessary to stress this point because the Community jargon itself has been extremely confusing. It has tended to reserve the term 'political' to describe co-operation in foreign policy. This usage has no doubt encouraged the idea that 'political union' would require such different institutions and different constitutional arrangements as to warrant developing new structures and procedures alongside the present Community.[13] On the contrary, the fact is that it is the very impact of what the existing Community has done in accordance with the treaties that has created the need for expanding the scope—and the political importance—of decision making in a Community framework. That the Community usage is at last changing is suggested by the Tindemans Report on European Union which goes out of its way to stress the need to unify rather than disperse the Community's responsibilities.[14]

The point is that the Common Market entails legal provisions that are not and, more important, cannot be politically neutral. That is because those provisions of necessity affect the distribution of resources not only among States, which is political in itself, but also among individuals, groups and communities. Moreover, given that economic activity is by its nature not static, they will have to be repeatedly re-adjusted, thus continually requiring political decisions about the distribution of resources.[15]

It is not possible in the scope of this study to support this argument with all the economic justification that it deserves. Economists themselves have been backward in dealing with the policy implications of the Common Market, as opposed to measuring its quantitative effects. The attention of students of politics has been alerted so far mainly by the assertion of economists, concerned with the future development of the Community, that the 'negative' integration brought about by provisions establishing the Common Market should now be complemented by measures of 'positive' integration. The argument is roughly that by liberalising the movement of goods, services and factors of production, the Community has taken away from State governments vital means of promoting

---

[13] That separate procedures should be developed for 'political union' has been a persistent argument of the Gaullists. See M. Camps, *European Unification in the Sixties*, (London, 1967), pp. 1–81. Its influence is still seen in the way co-operation in foreign policy is conducted (by Conferences of Foreign Ministers rather than by the Council itself) and in the role of the 'European Council' consisting of heads of governments, see: A. Morgan, *From Summit to Council: Evolution in the EEC*, (London, 1976); European Parliament, Report of the Political Affairs Committee, Luxemborg, Doc. 427/77. See also pp. 55–62.

[14] EC Commission, Bulletin of the European Communities, supplement 1/76, pp. 14–15.

[15] This argument must be carefully distinguished from the once prevalent academic view that economic integration would lead automatically to political union by a process called 'spillover', a solecism equalled only by the term 'spillback' used to describe the evidence that refuted the theory of 'spillover'. See E. Haas, *The Uniting of Europe*, 2nd ed., (Standford, Col. 1968), pp. xi–xix; Lindberg and Scheingold, *op. cit.*, pp. 101–41. For a major criticism of that approach see Hoffman, *op. cit.* My argument here is that economic integration has political significance enough but that there is nothing automatic about its effects on political institutions.

economic and social objectives like stable prices, full employment, economic welfare and growth. Therefore, new collective means of aiming at these goals should be created in the Community.[16] The Commission's attitude and to some extent the development of the Community itself in the 1970s in areas such as regional and social policy, have reflected the influence of this argument.[17]

Generally, the inadequacy of the Common Market from the point of view of positive integration helps to explain the recent concentration of the Community on movement towards an economic and monetary union. There are important differences about what this should mean in practice.[18] Not surprisingly, the implication that key aspects of economic policy making should be decided in a Community forum has been resisted by the Member States, though important steps to set up a European Monetary System are now being taken. It is often supposed that a major obstacle to economic union is the need for a new transfer of powers to the Community. But a greater problem in fact is that the decisions involved can be made only by considering certain fundamental questions about the role of government in the economy and about the nature of the economy itself. In modern circumstances that requires a complex and highly developed political process.

Among other things a political process based primarily on bargaining among State governments may well not be adequate.[19] The Community has in fact already produced 'positive' integration, particularly in the form of the common agricultural policy but the experience so far has been that economic intervention by Community authorities is accepted only in ways that satisfy powerful State interests, especially when they are backed by highly organised producer interests. I shall return to the institutional consequences of this experience later but the point leads conveniently to the second main reason why the Community's economic development must affect the existing political order.

Alongside the continuing business of establishing and regulating the Common Market (and a good deal of work is still required to harmonise relevant national rules and practices), the day-to-day work of the Community is largely that of seeking agreement either on implementing or on formulating specific 'common policies': agriculture, external trade relations, overseas development, transport, labour and social affairs, monetary affairs, the environment, education and

---

[16] See J. Pinder, Positive integration and negative integration, in *The World Today,* Vol. 24 1968, pp. 88–110; R. J. Harrison, *Europe in Question*, (London, 1974), pp. 184–209; L. Tsoukalis, *The Politics and Economics of European Monetary Integration*, (London, 1977), especially pp. 11–31, 169–76.

[17] Tsoukalis, *op. cit.*, pp. 82–168; EC Commission, Eleventh General Report, 1977, Brussels Feb. 1978, pp. 17–25; EC Commission, Programme for 1977, Brussels, Feb. 1977; EC Commission, Bulletin, supplement 5/75, pp. 14–21, 29–30 (where the terms 'passive' and 'active' integration are used rather than 'negative' and 'positive'); M. Shanks, The EEC—a Community in search of an identity in *The Thee Banks Review*, Sept. 1977, No. 115.

[18] See Tsoukalis, *op. cit.*; EC Commission, Report of the Study Group 'EMU 1980', Brussels March 1975; M. Shanks, *European Social Policy, Today and Tomorrow*, (Oxford, 1977); Federal Trust, *Economic Union in the EEC*, (London, 1975); G. Magnifico and A. Williamson, *European Monetary Integration*, (London, 1972).

[19] A point fully accepted by the Commission, see Bulletin, supplement 5/75, p.13.

science, energy, regional development and so on. (The differentiation is largely matched in both the specialisation of the Commission's internal structure and in that of the Council's changing ministerial composition according to subject matter.)

The approach has no doubt been greatly influenced by the idea that functional integration (in the sense of creating common instruments of policy only where particular interests can be seen to require it) is likely to be more feasible than trying to confront the complex political issues that are bound to arise when public policy is treated in general terms. So it is perhaps not surprising that a recent study of Community policy making in selected fields should conclude that the Community's approach to integration is far from uniform. Different results are obtained, and different methods are shown to be appropriate, from one sector or policy aspect to another. Because some sectors and policy aspects are more integrated than others and because the Community has not obtained the power to make general, strategic decisions about economic policy (or about public policy as a whole), the participating States seem to be creating not a new body politic with a supranational or federal government so much as indeterminate 'transnational' arrangement marked by:

> growing decentralisation with power slipping from the group of governments but not accumulating in any one place, certainly not totally in the hands of international organisations.[20]

However, the sector approach offers no escape in the end from the intensely political problems of co-ordinating different sectors, or of deciding overall economic strategy. Indeed, by making these problems worse it threatens to make the Community, not only irrelevant to the Member States in resolving their real economic problems like inflation and unemployment, but actually obstructive by preventing the States from using certain economic measures autonomously. So the Community must move constructively towards a more co-ordinated approach, not in order to promote more European integration, but simply because otherwise the States will be obliged to revert to autonomous action to protect their national economies by using the various restraints on trade that the Community was set up to abolish. On the other hand, both the Community itself and the States' governments individually have been very much aware of the risks involved, which explains why such a major effort has been made, beginning mainly with the summit meeting at the Hague in 1969, to develop means of co-operation both in general economic policy and in foreign policy, culminating in the declaration on European Union at the Paris summit of 1972.[21]

New challenges—interdependence, external relations and enlargement
Important developments since the Community's beginning have further increased its political significance. One is the economic 'interpenetration'

---

[20] Wallace, Wallace and Webb, *op. cit.*, p. 24, see also pp. 301–25. The concept 'transnational' comes mainly from R. Keohane and J. Nye (eds.), *Transnational relations and world politics*, (Harvard 1972).

[21] See Pryce, *op. cit.*, pp. 141–70.

brought about by the Common Market itself and the fact that some sectors, particularly agriculture, are now more or less integrated. Another development concerns general changes in technology that force certain sections of European industry to operate on a larger scale in order to remain competitive in the world economy.[22] Yet another is the growing interdependence of the world economy in general and of the advanced, industrialised countries in particular. This makes it essential in formulating and administering policies in the Community to take account of the effects on the world at large and of its reactions.[23]

Meanwhile, there have been corresponding developments in the way the Member States choose, or are obliged, to order their economic priorities. For one thing, concern for rapid economic growth by liberalising trade, which made it possible to accept the different sacrifices required in establishing the Common Market, has turned into a more complicated set of policy objectives concerned with maintaining stability in price levels and monetary values, spreading wealth both regionally and socially, protecting environmental and consumer interests and coping with unemployment especially that which is often described as 'structural'. For another, a 'new world economic order' has emerged. In many respects what seemed to be a relatively stable system established at the end of the second world war has actually been replaced by a new 'disorder', especially in monetary affairs.[24] At the same time the advanced, industrialised countries have been forced to re-assess their values, in the face of shortages of essential raw materials, the need to accept competition from newly industrialised developing countries and the acute problems in the third world.[25] Not only is it felt that the Community provided by the treaties was not designed for such circumstances but the common interests of the Member States are now seen as both more extensive and less specific.

One respect in which the Community has come to recognise its responsibilities towards the world outside is in its preparedness to consider a further enlargement of its membership to include Greece, Portugal and Spain. The Community's political significance would be further increased by such a step, since a major reason for the enlargement would be to strengthen liberal democracy in the countries concerned.

The previous enlargement, however, undoubtedly reduced the Community's ability to keep its basic aims and principles while adapting to new challenges.

---

[22] See C. Layton, European Advanced Technology, (London, 1970); Sir Bernard Burrows, G. Denton and G. Edwards (eds.) Federal Solutions to European Issues, (London, 1977), pp. 108–21, 211–20; for the effects of integration on the Member States' economic interdependence, see: Tsoukalis, op. cit., pp. 51–81; S. V. A. Cairncross, Economic Policy of the European Community, (London, 1974), pp. 1–30; M. Kohnstamm and W. Hager, A Nation Writ Large? (London, 1973), pp. 27–32; R. N. Cooker, The Economics of Interdependence, (New York, 1968); F. Perroux 'Indépendance' de l'économie nationale et interdépendance des nations, (Paris, 1969).

[23] Kohnstámm and Hager, op. cit.; R. Mayne (ed.), Europe Tomorrow, (London, 1972), pp. 35 ff. See also F. A. M. Alting von Geusau, Beyond the European Community, (Leyden, 1969); Burrows and Denton, op. cit. pp. 198–220.

[24] Kohnstamm and Hager, op. cit., especially pp. 22–82; Tsoukalis, op. cit., pp. 31–51; Cooker, op. cit.; Perroux, op. cit.

[25] Kohnstamm and Hager, op. cit., pp. 195–247.

48

Admitting Greece, Portugal and Spain would mean absorbing countries facing problems of economic development and accommodating even greater diversity of language, culture, politics and administrative tradition. The process by which the divergent interests of the original six States could be reconciled to form the Common Market has been disrupted already by the enlargement of 1973 and will be further strained if yet three more States participate.[26]

All these developments make the same vital demand on the Community. They require mature means of defining, supporting and carrying out general policy, not only a policy capable of being accepted in the common interest, but also one relating specialised sectors to each other and providing an accepted yardstick for Community intervention in them. Such a demand is rarely met adequately even in the government of long established nation states, and then only with difficulty. But there is no point in fudging the Community's political needs: in this sense it is bound by the same general rules that apply ultimately to governments everywhere.

Integrating particular sectors, which is what setting up 'common policies' seems to mean, is not an adequate response to the new problems. Nor is it where the Community's political contribution is likely to lie. The relative weakness of Community intervention in some aspects of social and economic policy compared to others may simply indicate that there is no call for it to be otherwise. The effectiveness of government should not be measured anywhere simply by the number of social and economic sectors in which it actively participates.[27] Indeed, the emphasis on specific common policies as a means of bargaining one set of national interests against another has already put the Community in deep political water. It will do so more as the interests concerned are affected more critically, as the international repercussions are more important, and as the number of participant States increases.

To take deliberately a controversial example, the Community has tended to defend its common agricultural policy, not on the grounds that it is an integral part of an overall economic strategy for Europe or for the world (though it arguably might be), but because to disturb the compromise that it represents might bring down the whole structure of the Common Market. We now know what can happen when an enlargement of membership itself upsets such a compromise, while circumstances are not favourable for simply adding a new integrated sector to satisfy new interests.[28]

In summary, what the Community's political needs amount to, therefore, is more effective means of democratic government. There is no point in fudging that conclusion by interpreting the Community's activities simply as a process of policy making; indeed, it can be misleading to do so if it leads people to believe

---

[26] House of Lords, Select Committee on the European Communities, 17th Report Session 1977/78, HL 102; EC Commission, Bulletin 4–1978, pp. 7–11.

[27] The inadequacy of the sector approach to common policy is brought out in Wallace, Wallace and Webb, *op. cit.* See the review of the same book by J. Pinder in *International Affairs*, Vol. No. 55, p. 124–5.

[28] Tsoukalis, *op. cit.*, 151–68.

that authoritative decisions to implement the Community's principles and aims can be made without exercising government at the Community level in conformity with democratic values. Similarly, the fashionable pragmatic approach is wrong in supposing that it is enough simply to balance one national interest against another so that the status quo is successfully maintained. It is as wrong as the mechanistic view which measures success in terms of a cumulative transfer of functions and powers from the States to the Community. I am not, on the other hand, saying anything startlingly original when I conclude that the Community needs more effective government. Many scholars and practitioners would say, and have said, the same thing but usually with the qualification that it is an unrealistic conclusion. What I believe is new and realistic, however, is my contention first, that the Community's principles and aims have always required what amounts to the exercise of government at a Community level and, secondly, that the need exists regardless of any prejudice for and against European integration.

For one thing, the needs I have identified and the conclusions I have drawn from them do not flow from the intention to create a 'European Union'. There has been some discussion of the Community's needs for more effective and more democratic government following the 1972 declaration on 'European Union', in particular, in the Commission's report on the subject where different models of a future constitutional re-arrangement are set out.[29] But the role of political institutions is relevant now and it does not depend on the proposal for 'European Union'. Indeed, the political needs I have identified are severely realistic, unlike the plans for 'European Union', which so far have turned out to be worth little more than pious declarations by the State governments.

For another thing, the political needs I have in mind are far more tangible—and complex—than the vague notion of 'political will' that has been appealed to increasingly in the Community during the 1970's. If by appealing to that notion people mean that the support of the State governments is necessary for any major developments in the Community, then they are simply stating the obvious.[30] But the problem is, as it has always been, how to elicit that support and maintain it in such a way as to ensure effective government and to do so, moreover, while respecting democratic principles. The idea of 'European Union' has itself fallen foul of the unreality of thinking in terms of 'political will'. For example, Mr Tindemans's report on 'European Union' does not do much more than suggest some future policy developments that would be compatible with prevailing views of the State governments and especially with the prevailing suspicion of supranational methods.[31] The Commission's own report on 'European Union' does go much further but it too recoils from making institutional reform a priority, on the grounds that 'institutional systems reflect political realities'.[32] But the very foundation of the Community and its survival through

---

[29] EC Commission, Bulletin, supplement 5/75, pp. 27–36, 41.

[30] See Sasse et al., *op. cit.*, pp. 345–61, 332–42, where the argument about political will is developed more fully.

[31] EC Commission, Bulletin, supplement 1/76. See especially pp. 15, 20–22, 24–26.

[32] EC Commission, bulletin, supplement 5/75, paragraph 86.

many crises of 'political will', show that political realities, on the contrary, flow as often as not from the nature of political institutions. If 'political will' means the necessarily transient and divergent attitudes of the State governments, it has never, left to itself, provided a way out of crisis and has had to be channelled through an institutional process and on the basis of underlying constitutional commitments. If such a process and if such commitment prove inadequate, then there is no point in appealing to the personal intervention of national political leaders at however high a level within the States or to the assessments of 'wise men'—at least for any significant length of time. It is also profoundly unsatisfactory from the point of view of democracy.

The role of the Community Institutions
Another way of stating the conclusions of the previous section is to say that the need to develop the existing Community Institutions, so that they provide a more effective and democratic form of government for the Community, is of immediate, practical importance. We do not need, however, to think in terms of an entirely new constitutional arrangement or to start building imaginary models in the expectation that one day the State governments will create by some conscious initiative a new political union.

In some respects the Community's institutional needs have not changed: it still has and needs its legislative powers, so that the consequences of the transfer of powers from the States remain; it is, and needs to be, dependent on its Member States in a way that requires the direct participation of their governments; it also needs means of direct political representation, though this is still the least developed of its constitutional features. At the same time, the new challenges that have been considered in the previous section demand further development of the Community's Institutions in certain concrete ways:

(a) There is need for better means of co-ordinating different policies and activities, reacting to unforeseen events, amending previous laws and policies and enabling the Community to act as an entity in international affairs.

(b) There is need for better means of settling differences among the Member States and formulating, setting and carrying out common objectives, while recognising that the issues the Community confronts are increasingly liable to raise vital political problems within each State.

(c) The need for political representation and organisation at the Community level has become acute, not least because the same issues also affect interests and ideologies cutting across the States and divided within them, including the very question whether or not the Common Market should be developed into a more positive economic arrangement and, if so, of what type.

Such institutional needs as these are faced in one way or another by all regimes, and especially by federal, rather than unitary, and pluralistic—constitutional, rather than totalitarian, systems. As I have suggested, they have been recognised to some extent in the way the Community Institutions were initially set up. They broadly match the functions that we may suppose were intended, respectively, for the Commission, the Council and the European Parliament, that is: executive functions, a function of representing State governments, and a function of representing the people. It is important to add a fourth need, which is no less fundamental to the Community, that of ensuring the constitutionality of the exercise of government and upholding the rule of law, corresponding broadly to the constitutional function of the Court of Justice and the basis of the treaties. One reason is of course that the Community is not intended to lead to an indefinite accretion of public functions and powers; there must be means of limiting the powers of government at both State and Community level. Another reason is that there must be fixed rules to govern the way governmental powers are exercised.

How far do the present Institutions fall short of these needs, and what improvements if any are required? The study of political theory and institutions will not offer us ready made models or easy solutions with which to answer that question. One fundamental reason is that the Community is an untypical political entity. However, political scientists have illustrated, if not always deliberately, just how the Community's efforts at governing have resembled those of established regimes. On the whole they have been reluctant, often justifiably, to use concepts derived from constitutional practice and theory in nation states. Certainly it is not enough to rely on constitutional law to understand the political process of the Community. On the other hand, discussion of the role of the Community Institutions has often missed valuable political lessons by deliberately eschewing conventional descriptions of political institutions. I shall consider here in turn the first two and the fourth of the institutional needs I have identified: and leave the third—direct political representation and organisation on behalf of the people—until the final section of this chapter.

The decline of executive functions

A number of studies of the Community Institutions have emphasised the need for what is often described in a vague and unsatisfactory way as 'political leadership'. They have also laid particular emphasis on the role of the Commission. Thus one major American study by Lindberg and Scheingold described in some detail how during the 1960s the Commission had deployed 'very special leadership skills' to bring about agreement among the State governments on common action, the prime examples being the decisions to set up the customs union and the common agricultural policy. The Commission had in fact relied less on formal powers transferred to the Community than on its own tactical and persuasive efforts, backed by its right of proposal and of participation in the Council's proceedings, as well as its status as 'guardian of the treaties', to display a 'high order of courage, independence, and political skill'. When such qualities were absent, the Community had been stuck with deadlock, inertia or unresolved crisis, either (as in transport policy, for example) because the Commission's 'leadership' failed, or (as in the dispute between France and the other States over-British entry) because the Commission's role was inadequately defined. It is significant that the same American study drew heavily on the imagery associated with federal politics in the USA, and particularly with the relationship between President and Congress. In other words it showed how legislation was made, and policy established, on the basis of coalitions and alliances forged as a result of bargaining procedures like 'log-rolling', 'side-payments' and 'package-deals'.[33] The same imagery has been used in other histories of the Community's development towards the Common Market stage.[34]

Other studies have concentrated on the fragility of the Commission's 'leadership', due not only to its own internal organisation but also to its lack of resources of political support other than the State governments. Many of the Community's later problems in fact can be traced to its general dependence on bureaucratic types of authority and on the lack of means of political organisation at a Community level.[35] The first three chapters of the report of the Vedel Group give an excellent account of the 'denaturation' that the Community's legislative and policy-making procedures underwent from the mid-1960s on to the early 1970s. The Group concluded that a 'quasi-diplomatic' process was in effect replacing the genuine Community Method, and that there was urgent need to restore the Commission's function of *arbitrage politique*. It related this function of 'arbitration'—meaning in fact something more than mediation but less than arbitration in the normal English sense of implying a judicial process—to the need for greater 'democratic legitimacy', going on, as the Group's terms of reference required, to consider a strengthening of the European Parliament. The Group's report pointed out that what was lacking was not some absolute power of government, involving a change in the balance between Community and States provided in the founding treaties, nor some form of coercion or enforcement of a distinct European view. In fact the Group put the role of 'political leadership' precisely as follows:

. . . 'the existence of a political decision making power does not dispense with the need for negotiation; but it increases the chances of its successful outcome.[36]'

In effect the qualities of 'leadership', considered in these and other studies[37] to be essential for the Community's effectiveness, are what in most national regimes are expected to be among the functions of what is normally called the 'executive'. The studies concerned have clearly assumed that they are intended by the founding treaties to be exercised by the Commission.

The role of the Commission has come to be seen very differently, however, by

---

[33] Lindberg and Scheingold, *op. cit.*, pp. 64–248, and see especially pp. 178, 180.
[34] See, for example, M. Camps, *European Unification in the Sixties* (London 1966); Wallace *et al.*, *op. cit.*, pp. 301–22.
[35] D. Coombes, *op. cit.*, pp. 294–325.
[36] EC Commission, Bulletin, supplement 9/73, Ch. III, Sec. 2.
[37] See in particular the recent detailed study by E. Poullet and G. Deprès, in Sasse et al., *op. cit.*, pp. 131–235.

the State governments themselves, and especially in Britain and France. Repeatedly one hears ministers of the Member States diagnosing the Community's main institutional problem as a need to bridle the Commission's overweening authority and power, not (as the experts seem unanimously to conclude) as a need to restore and even extend them. It is not that the national governments under estimate the role of political leadership in the Community—rather the reverse. But they have increasingly come to regard it as a quality that should be sought not from the Commission but from the representatives of the State governments themselves. Three important developments in the role of those representatives, however, have restricted the performance of an executive function at Community level.

The first, which has already been described in this study, is the practice of a right of veto established by the State governments since 1965.[38] Clearly the suspension of the rule of majority voting in the Council limits the Commission's ability to build coalitions and promote compromise among the government representatives, using its power of initiative and its power to submit revised proposals under article 149.[39] More important, however, is the way a right of veto has been extended to cover not just the Council's consideration of new measures but also the preparatory stages before the ministers are even asked to consider a proposal. As a result the Commission is invariably obliged to clear its proposals with all the participating governments in advance negotiating at the level of civil servants and technicians.

This leads to the second development which is the vastly increased power of officials temporarily or permanently representing State governments at a Community level. It is now in effect not the Commission but State government officials, especially in the now formally recognised Committee of Permanent Representatives (COREPER), who usually determine what proposals shall come before the ministerial representatives in the Council for consideration. The extensive application of a right of veto also means that the Council has been increasingly reluctant to try to resolve differences among its members on its own, and increasingly prone to pass proposals back to official levels for further 'preparation' as a way of evading political decisions. The sort of *immobilisme* and entrenchment of special interests that ensue are strikingly similar to what has been described disparagingly as the sort of anarchic 'government-by-assembly' that is meant to characterise regimes with a weak and unstable executive like the French Fourth Republic or the present Italian Republic. One major consequence of such a system is that when decisions are reached, it is invariably by default or as an urgent last resort, without adequate co-ordination and without sufficient regard either for the general interest or the future effects. It is in other words in its inter-governmental procedures—not in the Commission—that the Community's so-called 'bureaucratic' defects lie.[40]

---

[38] See pp. 22–23, and for an account of how the practice came about, see Richard Mayne, *The Institutions of the European Community*, (London 1968), pp. 42–51.

[39] See Ch. II, pp. 20–21.

[40] See particularly Sasse, *op. cit.*, pp. 180–221, and on 'bureaucracy', see p. 335.

Partly in recognition of these deficiencies, a third development, particularly during the 1970s, has been to create a sort of hierarchy in the Council's own structure. The meetings of foreign ministers in the Council have come to act as a 'General Council' intended to co-ordinate, and to some extent direct, the specialised meetings of ministers of finance, agriculture, trade, transport and so on. More significantly, at a higher level of co-ordination and initiative, the heads of State governments have themselves adopted the practice of meeting regularly (now three times a year) in what has been known since 1974 officially as the 'European Council'. The precise constitutional status of these meetings of heads of government is far from clear. In some respects they seem to constitute an extra-constitutional diplomatic conference of State governments, sometimes substituting for the regular procedures provided by the treaties, sometimes supplementing them, and sometimes authorising their extension beyond the scope of the treaties.[41] In view of the way the existing institutional means have proved inadequate, the intervention of heads of governments has come to serve what most agree are vital functions. It has helped to break deadlocks arising among ministers or officials at lower levels, as over the introduction of direct elections or in relation to more day-to-day matters like the Community budget. It has produced new initiatives such as the recent moves to establish a European Monetary System. It has also served to increase co-operation in wider spheres like foreign policy, and to some extent to get the State governments to treat different sectoral activities in relation to each other and to a view of the Community's future development.

The increasing reliance on meetings of heads of governments, however—whether acting formally as the Council itself or providing an informal, extra-constitutional forum for improving understanding—has certain unavoidable limitations. Not only are heads of government overburdened already with domestic State responsibilities but their growing responsibility for Community business demands greater centralisation within State governments. It is not always possible to attain the necessary degree of centralisation, especially in coalition governments or those with minority support in a State parliament. Even when it is possible, the result tends to be a hardening and a narrowing of a government's stance in Community affairs. In general, policy making procedures within the State governments are inclined to emphasise a short term view of Community action, to stress the defence of special interests and therefore actually to increase the need for initiative, mediation and co-ordination from a Community level. The initiatives produced by the intervention of heads of governments are spasmodic and unco-ordinated and tend all too often to take the form of vague declarations expressed in communiqués or press statements of dubious legal validity and little eventual practical effect. While events like 'fire-side chats' may improve communication among the prime ministers or presidents themselves, the resulting good will is slow to spread to other ministers or to result in effective decisions.[42]

---

[41] See A. Morgan, *op. cit.*, pp. 67–74.
[42] See the Colloquium on the European Council, Association des Instituts d'Études Européennes, Louvian-la-Neuve, 6 and 7 October 1977.

In fact none of these developments in the role of representatives of State governments seems to compensate for the decline of the Commission's executive functions. That decline can be traced ultimately to two factors: the Commission's lack of the means of obtaining political direction independent of the State governments themselves; and the limitation of its powers of initiative, mediation and defence of the common interest to matters specifically provided in the treaties. If these constraints could be overcome—and I shall refer to some possibilities later—then the role of State government representatives could be organised in a much better way. For it is increasingly apparent that the demands being placed on the machinery of the Council are excessive. Its ability to co-ordinate its own decisions, to observe a fixed timetable, to resolve differences among its members, is intrinsically limited because its members are at the same time expected to reflect the interests and attitudes of their various 'constituents': the Member States themselves. It is unrealistic to look to such an institution for coherent and continuous leadership, or the formulation and expression of a unified view. It is wrong, therefore, to compare the Council with the Cabinet or Council of Ministers of a national regime, acting with collective responsibility and performing executive functions. The more the Council is seen in such a way, the greater are the problems of providing adequate representation of the States at a Community level.

The representation of State governments
The negative effects on democracy of these developments in the representation of State governments should not be under estimated. The right of veto has been defended as a means of enabling ministerial representatives in the Council to delay decisions that have not been previously approved by national parliaments. However, it is extremely doubtful whether it is as important as is sometimes claimed for ensuring adequate consideration of Community proposals at a State level. What really determines the scope for influencing Community decisions from within the States is the normal relationship between the central government there and representative institutions, not Community procedures themselves.[43] What the right of veto certainly means in its extended form, however, is that it is extremely difficult to bring about changes in the Community. The right of veto can be used as an instrument to maintain the status quo but even then it is extremely clumsy and may be self defeating, because it makes it very difficult to form coalitions in defence of a particular policy or set of policies. The extent of delegation to official governmental representatives, moreover, puts the process of dealing with Community business at an even further remove from the representative process in the Member States, or for that matter anywhere.

In general, leaving more of the responsibility for effective government at a Community level to the representatives of State governments requires excessive centralisation at State level and impedes public accountability. It increases the discretion that has to be given both to ministers and to civil servants of the central

---

[43] Sasse, *op. cit.*, pp. 42–66, 310–31; J. Fitzmaurice, *The European Parliament*, (London, 1978), pp. 27–51; The Hansard Society, *The British People: Their Voice in Europe*, (London, 1977).

government and so extends their power relative to representative institutions within each State. Recent studies of the way State governments find it necessary to make policy in relation to the Community and organise their representation there have shown that these are inevitable consequences of relying on inter-governmentalism to such an extent while the Community has developed both its political importance and its scope.[44]

At the same time the Council's representative function continues to be vital. Just like the Commission's executive functions, it would have to be invented if it did not exist. It is undoubtedly becoming all the more important as the Community tries to deal with monetary and general questions for which a regulatory type of decision is much less appropriate than *concertation*. What that means is obtaining agreement, not by establishing a hierarchy of rules, but by directly involving those affected.[45] In view of the continuing importance of the Member States' governments to the Community's development and of the growing importance of concertation as opposed to regulation, the Community must continue to involve representatives of the governments of the States as direct participants. In a sense, then, the Council should be compared with the Bundesrat of the Federal German Republic, rather than with executive Cabinets or Councils of Ministers. Indeed, if executive functions could be performed more effectively by the Commission, then the Council might be able to become far more efficient as a representative institution. Or, to put it a better way, its present idiosyncracies might be far more tolerable. Take, for example, the general preference of the governments to be represented by different ministers according to the subject matter of a Council meeting, a characteristic that prevents the Council among other things from having a consistent and uniform membership. The failure of the proposal that governments should be represented by special ministers for European affairs (perhaps the permanent representatives raised to ministerial status) shows that the participation of governments needs to be far more direct than in a typical federal second chamber.[46] However, the demands on national ministers would be unbearable if they were required to exercise a double mandate as members both of a national and of a European political executive.

Moreover, the Council's structure could be further developed on hierarchical lines, with the Foreign Ministers acting as a General Council in relation to the specialised meetings of other ministers. There is also every reason for the heads of governments to meet from time to time as members of the Council. Furthermore, the inevitable role of permanent representatives and other official governmental delegates could be regularised by empowering ministers constitutionally to delegate their powers as members of the Council. The Council could then develop its structure to include a system of specialised committees and sub-committees to replace the confused and clumsy arrangement of official commit-

---

[44] Sasse, *op. cit.*, pp. 5–86, 113–7; Wallace et al., *op. cit.*, pp. 33–66; Hansard Society, *op. cit.*

[45] See G. Ionescu (ed.), *Between Sovereignty and Integration*, (London, 1974), pp. 20–22, 86–99.

[46] On proposals for 'European Ministers' and particular national experiments with the same, see Helen Wallace, *National Governments and the European Communities*, (London, 1973); Sasse, *op. cit.*, pp. 66–73.

tees and working parties that is vital to its work but now largely evades effective co-ordination and control. This would not and should not supersede the activity of pre-legislative consultation of national civil servants by the Commission. It would, however, draw out in constitutional terms the logic of the Council's function as a representative institution, while recognising the practical limitations it implies.

This is not the place to take further the logic of this approach to reforming the Council's structure and procedure. For example, should the Council still meet exclusively in private session? Given the continuing importance of delicate negotiation among national governments' representatives, privacy will surely continue to have a valuable function in the Council. However, greater publicity about the significance of Community measures, about their likely effects and about the play of interests for and against them, is much more likely if the separation of powers among Community institutions can be more firmly established. More will be said on this point in Chapter V.

It is worth stressing that any further enlargement of the Community's membership would clearly make it even more fanciful to look to a body representing States' governments for effective exercise of functions demanding a high degree of cohesion, flexibility and internal discipline. It would, however, place an even higher premium on establishing effective means of articulating a common interest, co-ordinating policy and delegating responsibility for implementing common policy.

The constitutional framework

Although there have been repeated references to the need in the Community's future development for 'discretionary power',[47] for 'a centre of decision',[48] for a 'centre of conception, initiative, mediation and administration',[49] for a 'major new authority',[50] and even for a 'European Government',[51] there has been extraordinarily little examination of what all this means in practice. The failure to look the problem in the face has produced ignorance, fear and exaggeration.

It is right to be loth to create new powers of government, not only because we may be jealous of the independence of our national governments and not only because we may doubt whether the supranational idea in Europe can be at all practical but also, and above all, because if we really want limited and democratic government we should look with suspicion on new government anywhere. The trouble is that, in spite of our vaunted democratic traditions, we have come to think of government only in absolute terms. Perhaps, indeed, it does not say much for the methods of government to which we are accustomed if the only form of political authority we can conceive is one that must be so overbearing as to be intolerable. Such a fear may be more understandable in Britain where there is not such a tradition of constitutional limitation of government as in other

---

[47] EC Commission Bulletin, supplement 5/73.
[48] *Ibid.*, supplement 11/70.
[49] *Ibid.*, supplement 9/73, Ch. VII, Sec. 2.
[50] Mr Roy Jenkins in the Jean Monnet lecture, October 27, 1977.
[51] Mr Willy Brandt in EP Debates, EC Official Journal, No. 168, 13 November 1973.

Member States. But are we so addicted to highly centralised government, at least in France and Britain, that we cannot stomach the idea of power divided between central and local authorities, and separated between executive and other branches? Certainly our national leaders seem psychologically incapable of conceiving worthwhile political authority unless it also promises limitless power. However, there is a vast amount of experience from which to draw in designing a constitutional framework that will offer some guarantee of effective executive leadership that is at the same time limited by direct democratic checks, by the power of independent regional authorities and by judicial review. The history of government in the USA, for example, is full of experience of the successes and failures of executive power subject to such limitations.[52] That country's experience of the last hundred years might well offer more evidence on the negative side for those who mostly fear a central executive. But there is also the experience of the Swiss Constitution of 1848 putting the executive virtually into commission, in that the Federal Council consists of a fixed number of members appointed for a fixed term resembling in these ways the Commission of the European Community.[53] Clearly the circumstances of Swiss government are not in major respects comparable with those of the present Community, and indeed no existing constitutional model can be entirely satisfactory: the Community is *sui generis*. The point here is that we might not need to look much further than the powers the Commission now has, short only of articulation and definition: the powers of corporate independence, of initiative, of mediation, of representing and implementing the common interest. To bring these powers to life two ingredients are lacking: means of direct political representation and organisation at a Community level, and the right to use such powers in general as well as specific terms.

Since the decision to complete the Common Market in 1969 the survival of the Community has been increasingly seen to depend on spasmodic expressions of 'political will' by the State governments, clothed in more or less vague objectives but given increasing authority in formalised meetings of heads of governments—what is now known as the 'European Council'. Such a remedy is unsatisfactory, not only for the reasons given above, but also because it leads even further away from the direction of limited, controlled and accountable government. Such an irregular inter-governmental diplomatic process, which pre-dates the treaties is, however, a sort of pragmatic reaction to the political needs of the Community as they have been identified here. It is above all a response to the exhaustion of the Commission's legitimacy, which flows partly from the fact that:

> those texts in the treaties governing Community policies still to be implemented (i.e. over and above those associated with the establishment of

---

[52] For postwar experience that is often strikingly relevant to the Community, see particularly R. E. Neustadt, *Presidential Power*, (New York, 1962), and A. M. Schlesinger, *Congress and the Presidency*, (New York, 1969).

[53] See C. J. Hughes, *The Government of Switzerland*, (London, 1957); W. E. Rappard, *La Constitution Fédérale de la Suisse*, (Boudry, 1948).

e

the Common Market) are infinitely less specific than the texts applying to Common Market policies. The Commission cannot rely on any precise commitments by the member states in the matters of the procedures governing non-Common Market policies, the time tables for their implementation, or the delegation of authority necessary for putting them into effect. It must therefore possess enhanced powers of legitimacy if it is to continue to play any truly active role at all.[54]

It is beyond the scope of this study to consider how constitutional means of enhancing the Commission's powers (and adapting its organisation accordingly) should be developed.[55] I shall confine myself to suggesting three existing means by which some progress could be made in the short term: broadly, through articles 235 and 155 of the EEC Treaty and the Community budget. Their advantage is not their orthodoxy. It is that for those who worry (as does the author of this study) about the survival of liberal democratic forms, measures taken under these two Articles and in the budget are subject, unlike decisions of the 'European Council', to four essential constitutional checks: the need for a proposal to be initiated by the Commission, the need for the approval of the States' governments represented in the Council, the right of participation of the European Parliament, and judicial control by the Court of Justice.

Article 235 can be used to enable the Council, after consulting the Parliament, to bestow general powers on the Commission to make proposals for new measures beyond the specific provisions of the treaties. The Council could use this basis, extending the logic of the article in the present altered circumstances, by acting only with the Parliament's prior approval (after allowing it a second reading) and by laying down subsequent procedures that made acceptance of the Commission's proposals dependent on its own and the Parliament's approval.

Article 155 can be used among other things to empower the Commission to exercise powers of implementation conferred on it by the Council.[56] The Commission is accountable to the Parliament for the exercise of these (and other) powers under the terms, above all, of article 144, that is, the Parliament's power to pass a motion of censure.[57] By extension that relationship can be developed into one of active responsibility of the Commission before the Parliament, as can the delegation of powers itself, into an act that the Council would not take without the Parliament's prior consent.

As we have already seen, the revised budgetary procedure of the Community does not yet provide for a sufficiently rational process of making expenditure decisions, partly because of the limited nature of the power of 'own resources', and partly because of the power remaining with the States' governments virtually

---

[54] In Sasse, *op. cit.*, pp. 228–9.

[55] See however the study of Poullet and Deprès in Sasse et al, on which I have drawn extensively.

[56] The relevant parts of the articles are: 'In order to ensure the proper functioning and development of the common market, the Commission shall: exercise the powers conferred on it by the Council for the implementation of the rules laid down by the latter.' See also EC Commission, Bulletin, supplement 1/76, p. 32.

[57] See Ch. II, pp. 20–22.

to impose expenditure decisions (like the common agricultural policy) by using their legislative power.[58] In fact, budgetary discipline does not so much mean 'cheese-paring' of particular items of expenditure as strictly co-ordinating legisla- tive and budgetary decisions, something which the Council has palpably failed to do. We have seen that the Parliament is already moving in the direction of using its enhanced budgetary powers to impose greater rationality, though the role of the Commission as the bridge between budgetary and legislative proposals remains crucial. In a wider sense, however, in spite of its presently limited size, the Community budget could be made to play a far more active role as a general policy instrument, even eventually 'as the main means of overcoming disparities in fiscal charges and public services in the various regions of the Community'.[59] In order to make the budget an adequate instrument of positive intervention to correct the imbalances caused by economic interdependence and to pursue goals of social policy and economic development, two particular restrictions would have to be removed: the limitation of Community expenditure to reimbursement of Member States' own policies; and the limitation on the sources of Community revenue and other income. The Council could use its existing legislative powers to overcome the first limitation while similarly extending the Commission's borrowing powers and could involve the Parliament by making these decisions in the ways already described in relation to article 235. Extending the Community's sources of revenue, however, would require an act of ratification by the Member States.[60]

It is unlikely that the use of treaty provisions illustrated here would be possible on the grounds of legal authority alone. We now approach, therefore, the consummation of this account of the future needs of the Community, since only on the condition that political representation and organisation are possible and include people as well as governments, can such an increase of executive powers be permitted. Whatever the urgency of the utilitarian arguments for strengthen- ing the Community's powers, they cannot be imposed for they can never be self evident. The Parliament enters, therefore, not in the role of Emperor but in that of Pope. The question of how much power can be drawn to the centre is also a question of conscience.

The conclusion towards which this chapter is moving is that, if it is to be able to respect its principles and fulfil its purposes, the Community must become a genuine body politic. That requires means of political representation and organ- isation at the Community level. It does not mean creating a 'super-state' out of the Community. Nor, on the other hand, does it mean that the Community can simply get by as a pragmatic inter-governmental organisation, either ignoring its effects on the existing political order, or expecting a body politic somehow gradually to emerge. The building of a European body politic, which began in

---

[58] See Ch. II, pp. 25–30.
[59] See Cairncross, *op. cit.;* pp. 56–58. See also EC Commission, Bulletin, supplement 5/75, pp. 19–22.
[60] According to article 201 of the EEC Treaty, providing for the introduction of own resources and used already in 1970–2.

effect with the foundation of the Community, requires neither absolute nor sudden measures but it must be deliberate and it must take account of the numerous choices and risks involved.

Practically all those who have tried to analyse and explain the Community's development have acknowledged that the border between an established polity and a pure international system is more vague and indeterminate than used to be supposed. That is illustrated by the way the Community itself has been able to get so far with such a limited measure of constitutional change. However, once concern for the values of limited, democratic government is introduced, the constitutional element has to take pride of place. Neither gradual 'integration' nor pragmatic 'policy making' are enough. The crucial question is precisely what sort of polity do we want.

The immediate problem in answering that question is to know if we should think in terms of the constitutional framework of the Community (broadly that established by the treaties and developed in accordance with them), or in terms of the sort of modifications that have been suggested and made, particularly in the 1970s, to lessen the dependence on supranationalism and develop more pragmatic methods. The growth of the 'European Council' as a kind of constitutional conference and the decline in importance of the conventional Community method have in fact gone a long way to transforming the system already. As I have tried to indicate, these developments on their own not only fail to solve the problem but in some ways actually make it worse. It may be argued that they have proved indispensable for furthering integration but my central argument essentially is that that is not the sole, or even the main issue. In so far as they do promote European unity, these new methods do so by paying far too little attention both to the questions of economic and social principle involved and to those of democracy. In fact, the constitutional framework provided by the treaties offers far more opportunity to satisfy these vital criteria than has sometimes been acknowledged. It may be inadequate, but we should at least begin by seeing what can be achieved within that framework.

Consequences for the European Parliament
The first consequence of these conclusions for the future role of the European Parliament is that the Parliament ought not to see itself as the only channel of political representation even when it is directly elected. Its role cannot be that of parliamentary assemblies in systems of government where the popularly elected chamber is supreme, or even dominant. Short of a major constitutional revision, the Member States will continue through their governments' representatives at least to share the power to approve the scope and content of action taken under the Community's authority and will probably continue to exercise an exclusive right of approval over certain matters.

We have already seen how the Parliament's attempts to assert itself have inevitably taken the form of claims to share with the Council the right to give approval to Community measures. I shall deal in Chapter V with the various means by which it can and may so assert itself further, in particular by obtaining the right of co-decision in general legislative as well as budgetary matters. But it is worth stressing here that the relationship between two such legislative authorities, while it must inevitably involve conflict on certain issues and over particular procedures, need not be destructive and would certainly not be unnatural. For one thing it will not necessarily, or even usually, be a conflict of one institution against another. A number of interests will cut across both bodies, will build themselves into coalitions and will in fact lead to a much more realistic and effective resolution of the relevant differences—ideological, social, economic, regional, national and so on—than exists at the present time. For another thing such a process of negotiation and compromise is not only typical of the way the Community has sought to exercise government up to now but can be regarded as essential to any system where a variety of opinions and interests have to be taken into account in the exercise of government. Indeed, it is not only with the States' governments that the Parliament will have to share its role but with the representatives of social and economic interests as well and possibly also those of regional interests within the States and cutting across them. I shall also return to the institutional consequences of all that in Chapter V.

Secondly, however, the representative role of the Parliament (like that of the States' governments and of other interests) cannot make sense without some executive authority, with policies and actions that exist to be limited and defined but with power to act effectively. A most pressing question for the Parliament and for the States' governments to decide, therefore, is their attitude towards the existing Commission. Do they intend to treat it as the Community's executive or do they intend to create some alternative? If the latter, then it will have to be a body empowered to exercise initiative, act as mediator, carry out policy objectives and otherwise perform the functions discussed above just as the present Commission was created to do.

I shall consider in Chapter V proposals for tying the Commission more closely to the Parliament by giving the latter the right to approve its appointment. For the moment, however, let it be remembered that the real problem so far has been, less the distance between Parliament and Commission, than the impotence of the latter. Its impotence flows essentially from its lack of the means of obtaining political support and the limited scope of its functions. One idea for increasing the Commission's political authority might be to make it the Parliament's creature and so transfer to it the democratic legitimacy that a directly elected Parliament will enjoy. But there are a number of problems in this idea, not least (following our earlier discussion of democratic and utilitarian approaches) that the Commission might be swallowed up in irreconcilable conflicts within the Parliament and become the victim of government by assembly. As it is, the more the Parliament's power is asserted in legislative and budgetary matters, the more stretched will the Commission's duty as mediator become—extending not only to differences among the governments represented in the Council but also to those between the Council itself and the Parliament. The question of what type of executive should be developed, therefore, suggests that constitutional issues may be at stake.

Thirdly, therefore, the Parliament will have to consider whether there should be changes in the present constitutional framework. Is that the same as saying, as some people have, that it should regard itself as a constituent assembly? There are some fundamental reasons why it cannot act as constituent assemblies have in the past. First, as we have already established, there is the fact that the Community is built on direct participation by its Member States' governments and they must be involved as sovereign bodies in any constitutional changes. Secondly, we do not face circumstances where revolution, anarchy or war have destroyed the existing basis of sovereignty: the States not only exist but effectively govern. Thirdly, the existing State regimes are unlikely in foreseeable circumstances either to disappear in their present form or to accept the need for a radical constitutional resettlement.

On the other hand, a major, innovatory constitutional resettlement of the Community may be neither necessary nor desirable. Many changes could be brought about by direct political means. What matters from the point of view of this study is that the basic principles and aims of the Community should be respected, including above all fundamental respect for the rule of law and for limited, democratic forms of government. Indeed, constitutional resettlement is unlikely to be desired or to be effective, unless it comes as a consolidation of changes already made by the evolution of political behaviour and conventions. Much of the continuing process of Community law and policy making implies some constitutional change in this sense, and that is precisely where the importance of the present constitutional framework and of the role of the Court lie.

Moreover, the democratic legitimacy provided by direct election, theoretical as it is and limited in ways I have already described, is important for the following reason. For one thing, in the short term it enables the Parliament to assert itself within the present terms of the existing treaties in such a way that the States' governments will find it more acceptable, less dangerous, and in some respects unavoidable, to alter their present collective attitudes and procedures. For another, in the longer term (although I still maintain that the Parliament could have done more in this direction already), direct election increases the opportunities for building the kind of body politic without which effective government in the Community will be impossible.

Above all, therefore, the Parliament must take a view of what sort of role it intends to perform, within the limitations implied by the need for effective government, the rights of the States, and the rule of law. To set out assuming that the absolute end, or even the chief goal, was simply further integration would be not only mistaken but also impossible, just as it would be to assume that democratic government could be assured by returning to a purely intergovernmental system. The issues involved can only begin to be resolved adequately with the participation of such an institution representing not governments but people. Only such a body can be trusted to accept the need for the sort of limitations on governmental power that have been considered here as an essential condition for creating it.

Much depends on the character of the directly elected Parliament as a political organisation, to which I shall turn in the final chapter. But I have excluded up to now a vital question which needs to be answered before a view of the future role of the Parliament can be attempted: what are the possibilities and limitations of the role of parliaments in view of the reality of parliamentary government that we know at least in the countries of Western Europe?

IV The contemporary role of parliaments in Western Europe

Introduction

The subject of this chapter is so vast that it could justify a whole book to itself, not to say two or three volumes. A full treatment would aim to trace the roots of modern parliaments in the history of liberal democratic institutions and in the history of political ideas, and make comparisons with contemporary political institutions outside Western Europe. What follows, however, is merely a synopsis designed only for considering the future of the European Parliament.

No serious discussion of the future of the European Parliament can ignore the prevalent sense of a 'decline' of parliaments in Western Europe. If the Parliament is to play a significant role in the evolving European body politic which previous chapters have suggested is essential for providing effective and democratic government of the European Community, then it is essential for it to get to the roots of that sense of decline, understand what it is that makes some people talk of a general crisis of parliamentary institutions, and decide what recent attempts to reassess the role of parliaments mean for its own powers, organisation and procedure.

For one thing, its own members after direct election will undoubtedly continue to conceive their own role and that of the institution itself in terms derived from national experience and tradition. For another, as we concluded in the last chapter, although the Community cannot be likened in political terms to an established regime, it is nevertheless attempting to perform functions that amount to functions of government at a European level. Indeed, its Member States expect it to perform those functions—even paradoxically those States where there is most scepticism or hostility towards supranationalism or to the whole idea of government being exercised at a European level. The experience of national political institutions is relevant, therefore, not because the Community should be seen as an attempt to set up some 'super-state' but because the widespread concern about its effectiveness and about its consequences for democracy implies that similar general rules should apply to its attempts to govern as apply to government elsewhere.

The problem is, however, that most practical discussion about the role of parliaments in Western Europe has been bedevilled by ambiguity and misunderstanding. Moreover, academics have come to use assumptions, methods and terminology that are not familiar or even meaningful to practitioners. Any attempt to look for models in national experience is, therefore, precarious. In fact, what this chapter will suggest is that before looking for such models, indeed before deciding whether that is the right approach, we must first ask exactly what it is that people mean by parliament. An initial step is to ask what contemporary writers mean when they talk of its decline.

The decline of parliament

What strikes one first about the common supposition that parliaments in Western Europe are in decline is that, in the words of Karl Dietrich Bracher: 'The phrase "crisis of parliamentarism" is nearly as old as the phenomenon of modern parliamentary democracy.'[1] Such relatively early authorities as Bryce and Lowell wrote of the 'decline of legislatures' with reference to the USA and elsewhere.[2] The popular, unqualified usage, therefore, immediately raises the question, 'Decline from what?', though that is precisely the question often neglected by those who base their arguments about parliament on an assumption of decline.

The fact is that discussion of parliamentary institutions invariably, if not inevitably, makes implications about wider political concepts. Views about the role of parliament in liberal democratic regimes are usually influenced by political ideas of varying vintage but, when recognised and made explicit, can be traced mainly to the political philosophers, Montesquieu and Locke, on whose conceptions of constitutional government much subsequent 'classical' liberal thinking and practice has sought to base itself. It is uncertain, however, whether a 'classical' model ever existed in fact or whether, indeed, the necessary conditions have ever been fully identified let alone found in practice. What is being described in many accounts of an alleged decline of parliament is a divergence of present reality from some imperfectly conceived ideal type.

However, what is firm in the extensive literature on the contemporary role of parliaments is that certain readily discernible tendencies in all liberal democracies have meant that parliaments rarely make effective use of their traditional powers. There are two main groups of tendencies both traceable roughly over the last hundred years.

First, and those most prominently adduced, are tendencies associated with the growth in both the scope and size of government. It is not only that the expansion of government has extended the physical limits on parliament's ability to influence and control it. The methods of government have become more specialised, technical and complex and its power more discretionary, less easily bounded within legal definition. Not only are specific legislative powers increasingly delegated to executive departments, but, as Blondel has aptly described, general legislation itself has declined in importance.[3] If spheres of government such as

---

[1] In problems of Parliamentary Democracy in Europe, in *Daedalus*, Boston, Mass., 93, No. 1 (Winter 1964), pp. 179–98.

[2] As quoted in Jean Blondel, *Comparative Legislatures*, (Englewood Cliffs, N.J., 1973), p. 5.

[3] Blondel, *op. cit.*, pp. 12–20.

foreign policy have always been suited more to executive action than to legislative control, the same is certainly true also of newer spheres like economic policy. Another adverse factor for parliamentary control is the growth of public expenditure and the enhanced power it gives to governments in management, and even direction, of national economies, as well as in influencing directly myriad industrial and commercial decisions. The extension of government in the economic and social spheres has also brought a multiplication of semi-autonomous state agencies, deliberately excluded in many respects from direct parliamentary control. It has also given governments as providers of vital social goods and services and as re-distributors of income and wealth, means of appealing directly and without parliamentary intervention to organisations representing social and economic interests.

That last tendency overlaps into the second group, which are associated mainly with developments in political representation. The chief of these developments, itself ironically propelled by the successful assertion of parliamentary democracy in the last century, has been the emergence and then the growth in importance of centrally organised, mass political parties. The official support of such a party and of its organisation is now virtually indispensable for effectively contesting elections by universal suffrage and the parties are usually able to maintain discipline among their members in parliament itself. As a result, the mass political parties have become an effective substitute for the traditional role of parliament in many respects and 'are certainly now the principle organs of political representation'.[4] The power of political parties has been fortified by widening acceptance of the idea of the electoral mandate, according to which elections are contested to choose between alternative party programmes and the winning party is not only entitled, but actually obliged, to carry out its programme to the best of its ability when in office. A corollary of that idea and of the contemporary role of parties, which has gained increasing ground in many European liberal democracies, is that the electorate itself should select the government and settle the main lines of its policies and actions directly through the medium of disciplined political parties, the member of parliament becoming a mere delegate.[5] In this way too much individual parliamentary intervention by members of parliament may even be seen as hindering democratic representation.

The contemporary idea of the decline of parliament, therefore, may be just as critical for parliamentary institutions as accusations of ineffectiveness made against them by the authoritarian Right before the second world war, or as the totalitarian Left's continued rejection of parliamentary democracy as a mere deception. The doubts now come not so much from opponents of liberal democracy as from its supporters. The case for decline is still at least unproven but one conclusion of the recent literature is indisputable. That is, as Blondel puts it, that:

---

[4] See Ghita Ionescu and Isobel de Madariaga, *Opposition*, (London, 1968), p.124. See also Bracher, *op. cit.*, pp. 346–8; Alfred Grosser, The Evolution of European Parliaments, in *Daedalus*, *op. cit.*, pp. 158–65.

[5] See A. H. Birch, *Representation*, (London, 1972), pp. 97–105, and *Representative and Responsible Government*, (London, 1964), pp. 121 ff.

'When theorists began thinking about legislatures, they faced a situation which was wholly different from the one that confronts most modern governments'.[6] In other words, a view of Parliament that does not take account of the effects during the last century of the growth of government and of the extension of the right to vote, must need extensive qualification before it can be applied in contemporary circumstances'.

Another important conclusion is that it can be inadequate and even misleading to describe the role of Western European parliaments in terms of their traditional powers. There are substantial differences from one country to another but recent commentaries on the role of parliaments in contemporary Western Europe all make vital qualifications about the importance of parliamentary powers of legislation, appointment and dismissal and control of the executive, budgetary approval and control and so on.[7] With variations and exceptions parliaments in Western European liberal democracies are still attributed with these general powers in a strictly formal, constitutional sense. Therefore, most recent studies of parliamentary institutions in Western Europe and elsewhere make a distinction between the formal powers of parliaments and their 'real' functions. The purpose of much recent research has been to determine by empirical investigation what it is that parliaments actually do—both formally and informally as well as both collectively and through their individual members. As a result, many students of parliament have suggested that what seems to be a decline of parliament should really be seen as the performance or adoption of different functions from those indicated by traditional powers as laid down in constitutions or described in legal text books.[8] Indeed, there is now a considerable literature on the functions of parliaments, presenting a view of their role which has proved influential among both scholars and practitioners.

The functions of Parliament

Many academic authors on parliament nowadays set about their task by drawing up a list of parliamentary functions.[9] It would not be so surprising that there are almost as many different lists as there are authors, if the reason were that there are substantial differences in the constitutional and political circumstances affect-

---

[6] Blondel, *op. cit.*, p. 13.

[7] See Bracher *op. cit.*, and Grosser *op. cit.* See also particularly the contributions in Sections I and II of European Parliament, *European Integration and the Future of Parliaments in Europe*, (Luxembourg, Directorate-General for Research and Documentation, October 1975).

[8] See Blondel, *op. cit.*, pp. 16–17; G. Loewenberg, The Role of Parliaments in Modern Political Systems, in Loewenberg (ed.) *Modern Parliaments: Change or Decline?*, (New York, 1971), pp. 1–21.

[9] See, for example: European Parliament, *op. cit.*, pp. 11, 39–40, 49, 121–4, 180; M. E. Jewell and S. C. Patterson, *The Legislative Process in the United States*, (New York, 1966), pp. 8–15; G. Loewenberg (ed.), *op. cit.*, pp. 1–21; M. Hirsch and M. D. Hancock (eds.), *Comparative Legislative Systems*, (New York 1971), pp. 1–21; P. Avril, *Les Français et leur Parlement*, (Paris, 1972), pp. 41–58; V. Herman & J. Lodge, *The European Parliament and the European Community*, (London, 1978), pp. 13–24, 64–73.

ing the role of parliaments from one country to another, even in Western Europe. However most lists produce different mixtures of formal, constitutional functions (such as legislation and appointment and control of the executive), functions that are primarily sociological (such as recruitment and 'socialisation' of political leaders or articulation of interests) and general functions in the political system (such as legitimation, communications and so on). Many authors draw, among other things, on much earlier accounts of parliamentary functions (in particular that of the House of Commons' functions in Bagehot's *The English Constitution*).

In general, it seems that authors are more anxious to reach some inventory of parliamentary functions common to all parliaments and applying to different types of political regime than to bring out the differences among parliaments even in liberal democracies. One consequence is that the functions positively identified as being essential frequently turn out to be the result of applying the lowest common denominator and may sound peculiar and unreal, not least to those with direct experience of working in parliaments. Another is that we may get a picture of the role of parliaments that is almost as formal and inadequate for describing what parliaments really do as the traditional accounts in legal text books.

One problem could be that, in trying to draw up as objective and generalised a list of functions as possible, people tend not to make explicit their own view of the political regimes concerned, or for that matter, their own view of politics. However, the differentiation of parliamentary functions from parliaments' formal powers has helped to confirm some conclusions that are indispensable for understanding the role parliaments actually play in contemporary circumstances.

Parliament or legislature?

One of these conclusions is that it is misleading to refer to parliaments as legislatures, or to regard the function of legislation as a defining characteristic of their role. This is more than simply a linguistic observation, since it is extremely important not to take for granted the assumption that the primary purpose of parliaments is to legislate, or for that matter that legislation in liberal democracies is primarily the business of a parliament. American writers are most prone to make such assumptions implicit in their studies of parliamentary functions. They may well be regarded as having some excuse given the stress both historically and in the present day in constitutional theory in the USA on the separation of powers. It is still disconcerting to see some American authors refer to Congressmen as 'our lawmakers' in the middle of explaining that law making is not really a Congressman's function, at least if one takes a sophisticated, modern view. In Western Europe there is no excuse for assuming that parliaments in all liberal democratic regimes are expected to perform primarily a legislative function. It is now fairly clear that some Western European parliaments play little part in formulating and introducing legislation, or in implementing it. Even their activities in deliberating on proposed legislation and in amending or rejecting it,

70

may be usually of little importance.[10]

In fact, the extent to which members of parliament play a significant part in different phases of the legislative process or have an influence on laws, varies considerably among the countries of Western Europe. It is not, however, enough in assessing the role of parliaments simply to quantify how much time they spend on legislation, the amount with which they deal, or even to estimate their influence on it. As we have already remarked, the importance of legislation in modern government is open to question in its own right.[11] Developing this point, Blondel connects the apparent decline of parliaments (or 'legislatures' as he calls them) with inadequacies in the 'classical' theory that the supreme power is that to make general laws.[12] Blondel draws the conclusion that 'because legislatures have been created in order to pass statutes, the procedures available to them are often in fact not very appropriate'.[13] His comparative study of parliaments in different parts of the world is largely concerned with examining how far they play a part not only in 'broad policy questions' but also as agents of detailed change and in relation to policies of intermediate importance. He shows that a whole range of procedures can be, and are, employed by parliaments in addition to law making.[14] Perhaps what we should ask, therefore, is why the function of legislation should be so closely associated with parliaments in the first place. The clearest and most helpful statement of the real position is still that of Sir Kenneth Wheare in a considerably earlier comparative study in which he makes a complete distinction between 'parliaments' and 'legislatures': 'This distinction in the use of words represents a real difference—a difference of view about the proper role of representative assemblies in the process of making the laws.'[15] Wheare himself quotes nineteenth century authorities for taking the distinction so far, in particular John Stuart Mill's dictum that: 'A numerous assembly is as little fitted for the direct business of legislation as for that of administration'. Bagehot too, while not wishing to deny 'the great importance' of the function of legislation, placed it last among his own list of the functions of the House of Commons and as of lesser importance than 'the executive management of the whole State, or the political education given by Parliament to the whole nation'.[16]

Contemporary students of parliamentary functions are not then telling us anything particularly new when they point out that legislative activity is not a

---

[10] See, Inter-Parliamentary Union, *Who Legislates in the Modern World?*, (Geneva, International Centre for Parliamentary Documentation, 1976); European Parliament, *op. cit.*, pp. 36–37, 38, 62–63, 77–78, 112, 133, 156; Grosser, *op. cit.*, Bracher, *op. cit.*; J. A. G. Griffith, *Parliamentary Scrutiny of Government Bills*, (London, 1974); S. A. Walkland, *The Legislative Process in Great Britain*, (London 1964); P. M. Williams, *The French Parliament 1958/1967*. (London, 1968), pp. 56–75; 84–89. On the restricted role of the US Congress in law making, see G. B. Galloway, *Congress*, (New York, 1953), pp. 9–11; D. B. Truman (ed.), *The Congress and America's Future*, (Englewood Cliffs, N.J., 1973), pp. 23–25. On parliaments in general, see Blondel, *op. cit.*, pp. 60–66.

[11] See pp. 67–8.

[12] Blondel, *op. cit.*, p. 13.

[13] *Ibid.*, p. 17.

[14] *Ibid.*, pp. 92–131.

[15] K. C. Wheare, *Legislatures*, (London, 1968), pp. 97, 112–4.

[16] Walter Bagehot, *The English Constitution*, (London, 1964), p. 153.

primary function of parliaments, at least not everywhere. The nub of the matter seems to be that law making is not intrinsic to the role of parliaments, although all parliaments at least in liberal democracies seem to have some part to play in it.

The question remains why law making should be considered, in different periods and in different regimes even today, as being essential to the role of parliament. One answer is that the rule of law was seen in 'classical' liberal thinking as essential to the defence of individual liberties, to the protection of private property and to the limitation of government. Another is that the role of law and legal procedures in the practice of government is still vitally important in some regimes. Parliament's role in law making may not be exclusive and may be shared with the executive and with the courts but law making may still be seen as the peak of government activity. The close identification of parliaments with the power of law making has probably clouded the issue of how laws are made and what is the significance of law within the government system. The study of parliamentary functions could serve to clarify that vital issue, though it does not take us further in trying to determine to what extent parliaments should exercise law making powers.

The place of parliament in the political system

This brings us to another necessary observation endorsed by the study of parliamentary functions, which is that the role of parliament can be understood only in relation to the system of government as a whole. That does not only mean that we have to take account of constitutional factors such as the electoral system, the separation of powers between parliament and the executive, the existence of a unitary or federal form of government, and so on.[17] Even more influential than those factors are characteristics of political life such as the number, nature and organisation of political parties and interest groups, the scope of government in relation to private activities, the degree and nature of its involvement in foreign relations, and the way in which the public administration is organised.

Of all the factors making the role of parliament different from what its formal, traditional powers would lead one to suppose, the nature and organisation of political parties are the ones most frequently and prominently mentioned in contemporary studies.[18] Parties, as we have seen, have come to determine the relationship between parliaments and those who elect them.[19] By this means they bring about indirectly 'far-reaching changes in the process of forming political opinion and the function of parliament as an organ for decision and control'.[20]

In Western Europe it is above all with specific reference to the so-called elective function of parliaments—in appointing and dismissing the members of the executive—that the role of political parties is most often seen as being crucial. The country where they have gone furthest in usurping the traditional power of

---

[17] On the effect of different constitutional restraints on parliaments, see Blondel, *op. cit.*, pp. 30–43.
[18] See European Parliament, *op. cit.*, pp. 18–19, 32–33, 50–51, 67–68, 117–9, 135–6, 156–66; Grosser, *op. cit.*, pp. 167–70; E. Sartori, *Parties and Party Systems*, Volume 1, (London, 1976), pp. 3–29.
[19] See p. 68.
[20] Bracher, *op. cit.*,

parliament in this respect is usually considered to be Britain. It is significant that the widely quoted Bagehot, while stressing that the House of Commons was 'mainly and above all things an elective chamber' and that this was its 'most important function', and while recognising the importance this gave in turn to the role of political parties, failed to realise the full significance of what he was saying for the power of parliament in Britain.[21] As he pointed out in a telling footnote which he wrote before the introduction of the Reform Act of 1867,[22] and, as one of his most distinguished editors points out, it was precisely the extension of the right to vote and the rise of modern parties based on it which led to the House of Commons losing its status as an 'electoral college' and becoming 'merely the forum of debate between well-disciplined political armies'.[23]

It is not only where one or two dominant, highly-organised political parties can command a clear and disciplined majority in parliament that the powers of appointing and dismissing the executive are effectively exercised by parties rather than by parliament itself. (Indeed, such conditions have not prevailed in Britain nearly as often as is supposed.) Even in countries like Belgium, Italy and the Netherlands where, in different ways, the support of more than one party is usually required to make and sustain an executive and where parties may be internally divided and undisciplined, the real decision about the formation of a government rests not, properly speaking, with the parliamentary assembly itself but with the relevant party leaders and even the party organisation outside parliament. Members of the parties supporting a particular government may be reluctant to bring it down for fear of the consequences of embarking on a new and painful process of government formation.[24]

However, having established that the role of parliament in practice will depend on different aspects of the system of government concerned, and above all on the character of political parties, we are still left with the question how far parliament's powers should be diverted or restricted. Existing constitutions and the existing organisation and role of political parties may depart from standards of parliamentary democracy and it is possible, therefore, to criticise them from that point of view. Later in this chapter, I shall try to re-examine what it was about the parliamentary assembly that made the so called 'classical' thinkers elevate it to such a prominent place in their vision of the system of government and I shall ask whether their views are not still relevant in spite of the constitutional and political factors that have limited the role of parliaments in practice.

Members of Parliament

A third essential task in understanding the role of parliaments is to examine their composition and to take account of their internal structure. Many recent studies have concentrated on the personal backgrounds, attitudes and behaviour of

---

[21] Bagehot, *op. cit.*, pp. 158–60.
[22] *Ibid.*, p. 150.
[23] *Ibid.*, pp. 37–46 (The Introduction by R. H. S. Crossman).
[24] See European Parliament, *op. cit.*, pp. 133–40; M. Grégoire, *La Particratie*, (Liège, Editions du Grand Liège, 1965); A. Manzella, *Il Parlamento*, (Bologna, Il Mulino, 1977), pp. 19–45.

individual members of parliament, on the internal customs of parliament as an institution, and on the way functions are divided among different members and groups of members, particularly between leaders and followers. Many studies have aimed less at understanding the role of parliament itself than at describing how members of parliament differ from other political actors in a sociological sense. Members of several types of representative assembly have been investigated in this way, including elected local authorities and State legislatures in the USA, and the results are not always of great relevance for parliaments in Western Europe. However, analysis of the internal composition and structure of parliaments has helped to mark three features in particular.

First, following closely on the comments made above on influence of political parties, the role of parliament depends on the different political attitudes of its members, particularly their allegiance to parties but also their membership of other organisations. It is also valuable to know how members became involved in politics, why they sought, and how they obtained, a parliamentary mandate, and what was their previous political experience. For example, a recent study of French deputies along these lines identified three main models of a parliamentary career in the Fifth Republic. First, there is the 'local notable', owing his political reputation to social standing, professional position or personal connections with a political party (for example, through his family): he is likely to enter his political career by holding a local elected office which he often combines (as do about two-thirds of all deputies) with his parliamentary seat. Secondly, the 'militant' is identified; his motivation is primarily ideological and he would usually start his career working for a political party or for a trade union or similar organisation. Thirdly, there are those deputies (about one in every five) who have had previous experience as members of a ministerial cabinet.[25]

Following such empirical research, we are getting now a much better idea of members' own attitudes to politics and parliament and to their own role, all of which can help to explain the parliamentary activities members perform and what they seek to achieve by means of parliament's powers.[26] The results tend to confirm that the activity of a parliamentary assembly is far from uniform and that its members use the institution for various motives and with different results. They have helped to illustrate that behaviour within Western European parliaments is so diversified that it is only with great care that we should speak of parliament in a collective sense at all. In particular, it seems to be fairly general that not more than ten to fifteen per cent of the members normally play anything like a fully active part in the work of an assembly.[27]

[25] R. Cayrol, J.-L. Parodi, C. Ismal, *Le Député Français*, (Paris, Armand Colin, 1973), pp. 115–7.

[26] See, for example, F. Debuyst, *La Fonction Parlementaire en Belgique*, (Brussels, CRISP, 1967); E. Gruner (ed.), *Die Schweizerische Bundesversammlung 1920/1968*, (Bern, Franche, 1970); A. Barber and Mr. Rush, *The M.P. and his Information*, (London, 1970); European Parliament, *op. cit.*, pp. 133–157. For studies with a primarily sociological perspective, see: S. C. Patterson & J. C. Wahlke, *Comparative Legislative Behavior*, (New York & London, 1972); Robert D. Putnam, *The Beliefs of Politicians*, (New Haven & London, 1973); O. H. Woshinsky, *The French Deputy*, (Lexington, Mass., 1973); G. J. Di Renzo, *Personality, Power and Politics*, (Notre Dame, Indiana, 1967).

[27] Blondel, *op. cit.*, pp. 89–90.

Secondly, we need to take account of what has been called the 'institutionalisation' of parliament as shown in its internal structure and procedures, although again sophisticated terminology and techniques have served mainly to elaborate what is already common knowledge to most students and practitioners.[28] For example, it can make a lot of different whether and how much a parliamentary assembly acts independently of other organisations such as the executive, political parties or interest groups particularly in the way its own organisation and procedure are determined. The way the internal organisation of parliament (for example, its arrangements for committees) permits members to specialise and to obtain personal status in particular subjects can also affect the way its powers are used. There is also variety in the way in which parliaments take decisions. Not only is it important to know whether and to what extent voting and other behaviour are consistent on party or other lines. Formal acts like voting in divisions, signing motions or putting questions can vary in their significance as means of expressing individual or collective intentions. Again, therefore, it may even be misleading to treat parliament as an institution in its own right. It may be no more than the venue for any number of political structures with more or less distinct aims and organisation.

Thirdly, it can be vital to know how leadership is exercised within parliament and how far it is divided between a government-supporting majority and an opposition. There has been an influential school of thought in Britain recently that sees the real distinction not so much between government and official opposition as between government and opposition leaders, on the one hand, and backbenchers on the other. Several types of opposition can be identified within parliaments, including Kirchheimer's 'Opposition in Principle'[29] and also a heterogeneous 'factional opposition', in which different members or small groups of members challenge the executive on diverse policy issues not necessarily following a party programme or ideology.[30]

In Western European parliaments, however, life is normally dominated by the fact that a majority of the membership (whether of one party or many) are committed at any one time to give general support to the executive. Parliamentary activity can still vary considerably according to the steadiness and solidity of the majority itself and it is often within the majority that significant parliamentary activity takes place. But the role of parliaments in Western Europe is not usually seen in terms of 'opposition of a whole legislature, collectively and individually, to the executive',[31] as it is still common to view for example the role

---

[28] On the concept of 'institutionalisation' applied to parliaments, see N. W. Polsby, The Institutionalisation of the House of Representatives, in H. Hirsch and M. D. Hancock (eds.), *op. cit.*, pp. 1–21. See also G. R. Boynton, et al., The Structure of Public Support for the Legislative Institution, in *Ibid.*, pp. 39–52.

[29] Otto Kirchheimer, The Waning of Opposition in Parliamentary Regimes, in *Social Research* XXIV, 2, (Summer 1957), pp. 127–56.

[30] A. J. Milnor and M. N. Franklin, Patterns of Opposition Behavior in Modern Legislatures, in Allan Kornberg (ed.), *Legislatures in Comparative Perspective*, (New York, 1973), pp. 421–46.

[31] *Ibid.*, p. 428

f

of the US Congress. That is partly why it is common to regard the formal activities of parliament in Western Europe as producing what is no more than 'a mock struggle',[32] or a meaningless ritual. It may not mean that activities of political importance do not take place using parliament as their venue but it has· done a great deal to reduce the significance of parliament's constitutional powers. All the same, the fact that its members may not all see the institution's role in the same way does not answer the question what that role ought to be.

In conclusion, then, what positive inferences can be drawn from identifying the 'real' functions, as opposed to the formal powers, of parliaments. The methods, the scope, the terminology and the specific conclusions all vary but it is possible to discern in most recent attempts to analyse the functions of parliaments the same overall perspective. This perspective presents the general function of parliament as providing legitimacy for an existing political order, even though the role—or, more precisely, roles—of parliament are seen as including not only support for the government of the day but also the expression of opposition to it. Many commentators for example draw freely on three functions emphasised by Bagehot: the 'expressive' function, the 'teaching' function and the function derived from the medieval duty of the House of Commons 'to inform the sovereign what was wrong'.[33] In other words, parliament's essential purpose is seen as providing communication between the people and their government:

'The function of the legislature is to provide a means of ensuring that there are channels of communication between the people and the executive, as a result of which it is possible for demands to be injected into the decision making machinery whenever they exist and for the executive decisions to be checked if they raise difficulties, problems and injustices.'[34]

Parliament's traditional powers of law making, budgetary approval and control, appointment and dismissal of the executive become therefore 'residual';[35] their significance lies solely is the fact that they provide a public forum at national level for the ventilation of grievances, for the open discussion of great issues, for political education, and for filling the gaps between general elections by providing a 'permanent election campaign'.[36] In contrast to the 'classical' idea of parliament, still expressed in many written and unwritten constitutions, as the seat of ultimate popular sovereignty and as the source of supreme political authority, parliament is now seen as a secondary institution.[37] To the extent that there is a revival of interest in parliamentary institutions among political scientists, it is in their functions of 'integration of the polity',[38] as 'a medium of two-way

[32] Bracher, op. cit.
[33] Bagehot, op. cit., pp. 152–3.
[34] Blondel, op. cit., p. 135.
[35] Ibid., p. 136.
[36] Ibid., loc. cit.
[37] See, for example, M. Duverger, La Monarchie Républicaine, (Paris, Robert Laffont, 1974), pp. 82–98.
[38] M. E. Jewell & S. C. Patterson, op. cit., pp. 8–15.

communication to achieve a consensus between rulers and ruled',[39] in performing 'a legitimating function for the larger structure of public authority' by the 'mobilisation of support'[40] for and against the executive authority, and as a source of 'regime stability'.[41]

This way of regarding the role of parliament is by no means so novel or so dependent on sophisticated research as many contemporary authors seem to suppose but it has important implications beyond the mere description of what parliaments do in practice. It does not present the role of parliament as an issue at the centre of conflict regarding the nature of the constitution itself and integral to the whole question of how and by whom government is to be exercised. Rather, it considers parliament's role in terms of its efficiency as a source of information, its topicality and transparency as a medium of public discussion, its value as a source of recruiting and training political leaders, its expertise and originality in checking the administration, and its possession of reserved but not active, powers designed to guarantee responsible government. This view matches a lot of the thought and action of parliamentary practitioners; it needs to be tested against a more practical view of the consequences of the 'decline' of parliament in Western European experience.

The reform of parliament

In most countries of Western Europe the sense of a decline of parliaments has led to much practical consideration of reform in the last ten to fifteen years. It is not easy to compare the reforming efforts of one country with those of another, because not only do the terminology and the concepts differ but also the circumstances determining the role of parliament. However, to a significant extent the conditions described in earlier sections have been present in all countries, and there has been concern within parliaments to adapt procedures and structures to suit them.

It is normal to emphasise the contrasts between, on the one hand, what is seen as the British model of stable, responsible government and polarised politics and, on the other, continental regimes in which the support of the parliamentary assembly cannot be certain and parliament acts as an independent entity in government. During the last twenty years, however, there has been a striking convergence, at least in the way the role of parliament is viewed. A brief and selective review of recent attitudes to parliamentary reform in some West European countries is given at the end of this chapter.

Certainly, in all the countries concerned, what I have called a functional approach to defining the role of parliament (and thereby to explaining its apparent decline) has been influential. Above all, it has shaped reforms actually implemented and served to provide common ground between those looking at

---

[39] G. Loewenberg, The Influence of Parliamentary Behavior on Regime Stability in *Comparative Politics*, Vol. 3, No. 2, January 1971, p. 178.

[40] Richard Sisson, Comparative Legislative Institutionalisation: a theoretical explanation, in Kornberg (ed.), *op. cit.*, pp. 17–38.

[41] Loewenberg, in *Comparative Politics, op. cit.*

the role of parliament from a position of executive responsibility and those taking a scientific view. There have been three general objectives recurring in most discussion of parliamentary reform in West European States:

Transparency. Everywhere there is concern both about parliament's disadvantages compared with the executive in access to information as well as about the 'cultural gap'[42] between parliament itself and the people. Procedures such as oral and written questions, interpellations, short topical debates, and inquiries by committees, especially by means of public hearing, have been expanded and emphasised. So have means of improving public access to parliaments and their members, in particular by broadcasting and televising the proceedings. Here parliament is often seen as less important, or less appropriate, as a venue for taking political decisions, than as a source of information and public debate. Much criticism of current parliamentary methods, therefore, implies that these should be less exclusive and ritualistic and more open and intelligible.

Professionalism. There has been a growing, but not universal, tendency to see membership of parliament as a career in its own right, though the functions of membership may still be viewed in several ways: as law making, control of the administration, political brokerage, social work for constituents and so on. Often against strong resistance, however, reformers have been pressing a view of parliamentary activity that would make the individual member more of a public servant, exercising relatively defined and specialised tasks, and less of a lay dignitary or notable embodying and exercising popular sovereignty. Accordingly, there has been stress on specialisation and expertise, not only in such structural aspects as the use of committees and the provision of staff and facilities, but also in the payment, hours and other conditions of work of individual members.

Rationalisation. One way of viewing the reform of parliament is to see it essentially as a way of reallocating parliamentary time to achieve greater efficiency. In all West European countries there has been a tendency to reduce the amount of time allocated to the apparently more ritualistic proceedings, that is to say, those where the outcome can usually be predicted in advance. This sort of reorganisation has affected legislative and budgetary procedures in particular. In financial matters it has invariably flowed from a belief that budgetary decisions are determined essentially by policy choices and that members' interest in public expenditure is nowadays less in imposing financial restraints than in obtaining the greatest return from expenditure in terms of social benefits.[43] In ordinary legislation it has been increasingly assumed that governments exist to implement a programme mandated by the electorate.

All three of these general objectives—greater transparency, professionalism and rationalisation—are pertinent ways of adapting to changed social, economic and political conditions. Where they fail is in justifying parliamentary, as opposed to other forms, of government in those conditions. The current stress on

---

[42] Loewenberg, *Parliament in the German Political System, . . .*, *op. cit.*, p. 435.
[43] See D. Coombes (ed.), *The Power of the Purse*, pp. 364–90.

parliament's informing and teaching functions has undoubtedly been influenced by the cult of communication and the mass media, in both the social sciences and in society itself. Can communication be regarded, however, as a unique function of parliaments, given the competing claims both in efficiency and popularity of the mass media themselves—claims which do much to account for the so-called decline of parliaments? In other words, parliament's role is increasingly being seen as that of a passive instrument, as two French scholars of parliament have insinuated by quoting Jean Cocteau's remark that 'Mirrors do not reflect enough'.[44]

The way demands for greater professionalism have been resisted in practice also shows that reformers may take too reductionist a view. Again the justification of parliament's role seems to expose it all the more to those who argue that what parliaments do can be done better by other means: by the public administration itself, by independent experts, by direct appeals from citizens to administrative agencies and so on.

Finally, independent members of parliament are rightly suspicious of deals worked out with executives offering better means of specialisation, and even greater influence in secondary matters, in return for speeding up legislative procedure and generalised commitment to government proposals. Parliamentary opposition needs effective means of procedural obstruction both as a direct means of influence and as an ultimate sanction. Efficiency is after all relative to the political ends parliament is supposed to articulate. 'Rationalisation' can too often mean simply removing parliament's role as a source of opposition. In fact reform is highly ambiguous: it can mean putting restraints on parliament rather than reinforcing it, and often the distinction is not even clear among reformers.

The fact is that concern about parliamentary institutions has been caught up in a more general sense of crisis—actual or impending—of liberal democracy itself. There are many threads in this development, and parliamentary reform may not be the one that matters most, if at all. Indeed, one general doubt about parliamentary reform is whether it gets sufficiently to the roots of the problem of governing advanced industrial liberal democracies. Moreover, the widespread dissatisfaction with parliamentary institutions may be in fact neither a quarrel with the role of parliaments at all nor an impatience for their reform. The real causes of complaint may be general circumstances such as social inequality, economic failure or the loss of international status, and the real defects may lie elsewhere in or beyond the political regime concerned. Parliaments get in the firing line because for various reasons they can be identified with the existing order; commonly, indeed, it is not the actions of parliament that are the intended objects of public criticism but those of the executive.

A review of attitudes to parliamentary reform suggests that, while some continental European regimes have been attracted by features of the so-called British model, in Britain itself the disadvantages of that model have been increasingly recognised. The resulting convergence might help to find common

---

[44] Avril and Feydy in The European Parliament, *op. cit.*, p. 72. See also Predieri's remark; 'Informazione, si, ma per farne che cosa?' in Predieri (ed.), *op. cit.*, p. 253.

79

ground at least in identifying what elements would be combined in an ideal form of parliamentary democracy. However, formal constitutional powers must be included in any such exercise, even though they do not give a complete account of parliament's role. If we are to find the essential causes of the apparent decline of parliaments, moreover, we must look to the realm of political ideas and recognise that what is seen as a crisis of parliamentary institutions is at least partly a result of sometimes fundamental doubts about the ends of government itself.

The idea of parliamentary democracy: variations and alternatives

What is really required, as I admitted at the opening of this chapter, is a reappraisal of the whole idea of parliamentary democracy. That is complicated by empirical differences over space and time and by the impossibility of tracing the idea of parliamentary democracy to one consistent, clear source in political thought. Moreover, parliaments are one means of getting and holding political power, so that they may be designed in practice to serve different ends according to the existing balance of political forces.

The most I shall try to do here is to show what is at stake in the idea of parliamentary democracy, by seeking to explain some of its inconsistencies and by distinguishing it from other ideas with which it should not be, but often is, confused. It is hoped that this will be some help in showing eventually that the idea might be applied more effectively in terms of constitutional powers of parliaments and their internal organisation.

Certain essential and distinctive characteristics of parliamentary democracy seem to be suggested by its several theoretical presentations and its varied application in practice. First, it implies a form of representative democracy, precisely what form being very much open to question and depending among other things on the type of electoral system, the formal rules governing political parties and so on, but distinguishable in particular from direct democracy. Secondly, it contains the principle of institutional opposition, which is expressed in Ronald Butt's attempt to capture the historical roots of parliament in Britain: 'the one constant function of Parliament has been to provide for consultation between successive English Governments and those sections of the community, or their representatives, which have mattered in terms of political power'.[45]

Especially difficult to define, as we have seen, is the third element, the commitment implicit in the idea of parliamentary democracy to the rule of law, meaning broadly that the actions of government and of private persons should be confined within known and accepted general rules. Although the relationship between parliament and government has been its most variable and uncertain element, the idea requires, furthermore, a form of responsible government, a helpfully ambiguous term meaning at least three things: government that is answerable and therefore to some extent responsive to public opinion; one that is nevertheless stable and therefore to some extent independent of public opinion; and one that is able to exercise moral judgement in making a balance between its responsiveness and its independence in the act of governing. Fifthly, the idea

---

[45] Ronald Butt, *The Power of Parliament*, (London, 1967), p. 31.

favours a collegiate organisational structure to a hierarchical one, that is, at the extreme, one in which, 'apart from the presiding officer, the organisation is wholly horizontal in character',[46] each member participating on equal terms. Finally, at different stages in its historical evolution the idea of parliamentary democracy has been identified with that of national solidarity, implying both national independence and the validity of seeking some collective view of the common good based on the national unit.

All these ingredients have been qualified in contemporary thinking to take account of variations and inconsistencies, and of lessons from practical experience. The question is how distinctive the idea still is and what is its relevance today.

Representative versus direct democracy

The role of parliaments in practice has been greatly influenced by the effects of universal suffrage and particularly by the rise of organised political parties to a dominant role in the representative process. To a large extent the cause is to be found in a growing preference for direct democracy often expressed as a belief in popular sovereignty. In recent British experience, for example, students of parliament discern 'a drift towards a plebiscitary approach to political decision making which clearly undermines the very different concept of representative democracy and decision making in a representative chamber.'[47] Indeed, not only in Britain but in other Member States of the Community there has been increasing application of the theory of the electoral mandate, a desire to polarise electoral and parliamentary politics (with the alleged aim of clarifying and simplifying the people's choices) and growing recourse to the referendum by governments to appeal directly to the people against the decisions of parliament. In interpreting parliament's role as a continuous election campaign, and as a passive channel of communication between people and government, many of the functionalist writers and reformers have tended in effect to adopt such an idea of popular, rather than representative, democracy. It is the latter form, however, that seems to be essential to the idea of parliamentary democracy, in which the member of parliament is seen quite consciously as a necessary intermediary between people and government; hence the fear that mirrors may not reflect enough. As to what the growth of popular democracy means for the practice of parliamentary democracy, we should be clear that a potential or actual conflict of ideas is at stake. In practice, West European regimes may be turning more to popular than to representative democracy, or they may be settling for a combination of both. But it is misleading to present the trend as a mere adaptation of parliamentary democracy to changing circumstances.

---

[46] Maurice Vile, *Constitutionalism and the Separation of Powers*, (Oxford, 1967), p. 337.

[47] John P. Mackintosh, in Mackintosh (ed.), *The People and Parliament*, (London, 1978), p. 3. S. H. Beer argues that such a populist view of democracy lies deep in the roots of the British Conservative and Labour Parties: 'both Tory and Socialist democracy reject parliamentarism', *Modern British Politics*, (London, 1965), p. 70.

Functional representation

Associated with the populist approach has been the growth of corporatism, which has deep roots in social and economic changes since the middle of the nineteenth century. It is manifested politically today in the vast extension of government in the social and economic sphere and in the growing direct influence on government of private organisations representing social and economic interests. Populism has encouraged the emergence of 'big government' by spreading the assumption that a democratic government is meant primarily to serve the people's needs for economic welfare and social equality (though other more wide ranging political ideas have also of course been at work). Belief in direct democracy has also helped to legitimise the procedures whereby in all West European regimes now, both the vital political decisions and masses of routine ones, are made by negotiation with organised interest groups, parliament normally acting as no more than a rubber stamp.[48] The result is everywhere a revival of the idea of functional representation, though the process has fed back into electoral and parliamentary politics by its effect on the political parties. As S. H. Beer has described the 'collectivism' of contemporary British politics: 'if "bargaining" is characteristic of the group politics of the new system of functional representation, "bidding" is the word for the mode of competition in the parallel system of parliamentary and political representation'.[49]

Parliament's tendency to become a secondary institution is therefore reinforced, because governments now try to meet opposition by a form of economic trading rather than by parliamentary politics. At the same time, the government's problem of reconciling opposed demands and interests is infinitely greater because 'the basic allocative power is now political rather than economic'.[50] To say, therefore, that economic means will be used to satisfy wants no longer implies a largely automatic and decentralised process but one requiring direct intervention by government. The decline of parliament as 'the centre of our national life', in Bernard Crick's phrase[51] should be traced therefore not to deficiencies in parliamentary procedure but to the success of ideas that are altogether different from that of parliamentary democracy.

Decline of the rule of law

Another manifestation of the same trend is what S. H. Beer has called 'the increasing specificity of the essential governmental decision.'[52] We have already met this feature of modern government in liberal democracies when discussing earlier in this chapter why parliament's legislative power had become so ineffective. The reason was seen to be, not that some parliaments in Western Europe

---

[48] To get an idea of the range of 'corporatist' organisations involved, see Daniel Bell, *The Cultural Contradictions of Capitalism*, (London, 1976), pp. 258–9.
[49] The British Legislature and the Problem of Mobilising Consent, in Elka Frank (ed.), Law makers in the Modern World (Englewood Cliffs, N.J., 1966), p. 37.
[50] Bell, *op. cit.*, p. 226. See also pp. 235 ff. on the concept of 'overload' of governments and on this see also, Michel Crozier et al., *The Crisis of Democracy*, (New York, 1975), pp. 163–4 and passim.
[51] Hanson and B. Crick, p. 275.
[52] Frank (ed.), *op. cit.*, p. 34.

(and elsewhere) are no longer (or never have been) law making institutions in the strict sense but that the principle of the rule of law itself has been weakened. However, this trend should not be confused with the tendency of executives to extend their discretionary or prerogative powers, by using financial, managerial or other forms of incentive and persuasion (as in the *concertation* of French economic planning). Nor does it reduce the dependence of some continental European regimes on legal regulations in public administration. What has happened is that government by the particular rather than the general has weakened the principle of the rule of law as a basis for the power of representative assemblies.

At this point, we need to be wary of misreading what has been handed down to us as the proper role of parliaments in law making. Parliamentary assemblies were in fact concerned primarily with controlling the conduct of government in a general sense and particularly by using control of finance, before theories of the separation of powers identified them so closely with law making, thereby causing so much perplexity today for students of parliamentary institutions who observe that in practice the law making function is not an intrinsic feature of parliaments. The point is that: 'A purely "legislative" assembly in the sense in which the theorists of the separation of powers conceived it has never existed'.[53]

The 'classical' liberal writers did not overlook the fact that governments do and must act independently of the so-called legislative assembly. Locke himself dealt with what he called the 'federative power' belonging to the executive, and arising in his day mainly in the fields of internal law and order, defence and foreign policy. The rule of law to him was essentially a guarantee of personal liberties against tyranny, a limitation but not an exclusion of the government's prerogative.[54] John Stuart Mill much later took the argument further by suggesting that a representative assembly is in fact 'as little fitted for the direct business of legislation as for that of administration', but he did not regard this as taking away the assembly's right to 'the ultimate controlling power':

'while it is essential to representative government that the practical supremacy in the state should reside in the representatives of the people, it is an open question what actual functions, what precise part in the machinery of government, shall be directly and personally discharged by the representative body. Great varieties in this respect are compatible with the essence of representative government, *provided the functions are such as secure to the representative body the control of everything in the last resort.*[55]

Mill may well have gone too far in down grading the legislative function of parliaments and in this, as in other things, exaggerated the purely educational

---

[53] F. A. Hayek, *New Studies in philosophy, politics, economics and the history of ideas*, (London, 1978), p. 101.
[54] John Locke, *Two Treatises of Civil Governments*, (Everyman edition, London, 1970), pp. 190–203.
[55] J. S. Mill, *Considerations on Representative Government*, (Everyman edition, London, 1972), pp. 228–9. My italics.

value of parliamentary activity.[56] We can assume that the theorists of the separation of powers played up the same function because they saw making general rules for limiting the activity of government as one way of giving a numerous assembly ultimate power over government, without making government impracticable. In Western Europe the legislative function is still predominant in some assemblies. We should not infer from this that in some parliaments the legislative function is restricted to 'Bill-reviewing',[57] or that the power ultimately to withhold consent to legislation is not a way—albeit indirect—of upholding the rule of law. Parliaments may not always use their traditional powers as well as they might in order to set limits to government activity, but this could be changed.[58] The pure theory of a separation of powers, requiring a clear division of functions, is certainly not applicable in practice, so that law making is an activity shared everywhere by parliaments with other institutions in particular the executive and the courts. We have seen, moreover, that it is especially difficult today to use general laws as a limitation on the power of governments, partly because of political demands made on grounds of democracy. Nevertheless, we must ask whether the idea of parliamentary democracy is compatible with any system of government other than that in which the actions of public authorities are contained both formally and materially within rules upheld by elected representatives of the people. The power to review, alter and reject proposed laws, therefore, and even to initiate them, is neither superfluous nor unpractical, though it cannot be relied on as the exclusive, or in all circumstances the most effective, method of keeping government under parliamentary control.[59]

Responsible government and the separation of powers
The 'classical' heritage also needs more careful scrutiny where it asserts in an apparent contradiction, on the one hand, the supremacy or sovereignty of parliament and, on the other, a constitutional separation of powers. It is not at all easy to trace the origins of the idea, reflected still in constitutions, that the representative assembly should be supreme. The main purpose of Locke and Montesquieu for example seems to have been to assert not this principle but that of limited government and a balanced constitution. In fact, in most eighteenth and nineteenth century liberal constitutions a system of elaborate checks and balances was provided to divide the different parts of government from and against each other. A major purpose of trying to prevent one institution from becoming more powerful than others was to stop the elected assembly arrogating rights to itself, on the basis of popular sovereignty, that might not only produce a tyranny of the majority but also make efficient government impossible.

---

[56] Like many academic observers of parliament today, especially some of the British reformers of the 1960s.

[57] Erik Damgaard's phrase in European Parliament, *op. cit.*, p. 43.

[58] See, for example, Gavin Drewry's contribution to Walkland and Ryle, *op. cit.*, pp. 70–95.

[59] Hayek and others would argue, in different ways, that the supremacy of general law should be reasserted as a way of reversing the corporatist trends of the modern liberal-democratic state; see in particular, *Law, Legislation and Liberty*, Vols. 1 & 2, (London, 1973 and 1977 respectively). See also, for the USA, T. J. Lowi, *The End of Liberalism*, (New York, 1969).

However, under the influence of populist and corporatist ideas of government and through the agency of modern political parties in particular, there is now a general trend towards a fusion of powers in Western European liberal democracies. This process can also be seen historically wherever parliamentary assemblies, as was frequently the case, rose to prominence as centres of opposition to an existing regime. Rather than settle for the status of an institutionalised opposition, the anti-regime parties or factions invariably sought to become the government themselves and were tempted further to seek to unify the power of the State, particularly through the organisation of political parties. This is why a separation of powers (as in the government of the USA), though intended among other things to put constraints on the power of the representative assembly, may actually prove the only way of protecting its freedom to make independent use of its powers. The alternative is to reduce it to a mere assemblage of party delegates seeking to support, and eventually gain office in, a government of one colour or another.

Therefore, although the notion of responsible government is more often associated with regimes in which the executive authority can be appointed and dismissed only by parliament (that is, where it is uniquely responsible to parliament), it seems in fact that responsiveness and stability may be easier to combine when the assembly and the executive enjoy a certain independence of each other. Government by assembly, where powers have been fused, produces government which is either so dependent on the assembly as to be ineffectual, or so preponderant in it as to be no longer genuinely answerable. This view of responsible government is tenable of course only if one believes it impossible for any party or other combination to come to power with the unique answer to social, economic and political ills, and only if one believes that in the circumstances of modern, industrialised societies the judgement of elected representatives is preferable to the mass public's 'decisions'. But such beliefs are surely fundamental to parliamentary democracy.

A further advantage in accepting a separation between parliament and the executive is that it helps to defend parliamentary democracy against the claim that it must lead to ineffective government, especially in modern conditions. The use of the term 'executive' in the traditional theory is in fact highly misleading, because what is called the executive in liberal democratic practice is not the organ of government charged with carrying out, implementing or executing plans, proposals and measures settled elsewhere.[60] An essential task of the executive, so called, is directing and ordering the general process of government, including taking initiatives, making plans, responding to unforeseen events and so on, so that the term 'directorate' would be far more appropriate. The functions of such a body (usually called confusingly in European practice the 'government') require it to take the main part in formulating and promoting new laws as well as in implementing them. It is also expected to exercise political leadership and to

---

[60] As Maurice Vile has shown, it is difficult enough to find any practical separation based on functions (such as law making/application of law, etc.), structures or processes (policy-making/administration), *op. cit.*, pp. 315–50.

arbitrate among conflicting demands and interests. Ideally, such an authority should not be so close to an elected representative assembly as to be stuck with the stark alternative of dominating it or being made impotent by it. Nor should it be so far from the assembly as to become entirely free from its influence or cut off from the realities of political power. It is the principle of responsible government, therefore, and not that of parliamentary supremacy, that is central to the idea of parliamentary democracy.

Parliament as an institution in its own right
The idea of parliamentary democracy is also badly in need of refinement in two other respects. The first is in its preference for collegiate rather than hierarchical authority, a principle that has been undermined in practice by three major developments. The fusion of powers that we have been considering creates a hierarchy in parliamentary assemblies under leading supporters of the governing party (who may, as in Britain, actually form the government) and leads to wider inequalities particularly that between frontbenchers and backbenchers.

Secondly, even an assembly that is relatively independent of the executive in determining its own organisation and managing its own proceedings finds it necessary in practice to develop a system of leadership, under a presiding officer and bureau, and to allocate formal authority to chairmen of committees, leaders of political groups and so on. (The history of the United States Congress is especially instructive in this regard.)

Perhaps the most pervasive development, on the other hand, is the growth of bureaucracy, which, through its effects on government in general, demands centralised decision making, specialisation of tasks, professionalism and reliance on career officials.

Some collegiality can still be preserved in the face of these developments, if it is backed up by formal rules of parliamentary procedure requiring personal voting and open debate. This is shown by the way backbenchers can exercise power even in a parliament as dominated by the executive as that of Britian, especially when they are supporters of the majority.[61] Rationalisation of parliamentary procedure, therefore, should always be watched with suspicion. The importance of formal, even if apparently ritualistic, powers as sanctions protecting the rights of individual members should never be under estimated. At the same time, the more the influence of individual members of parliament comes to depend on specialisation and professional skills—their own or other people's—that is, on work in offices rather than in a public arena (and the arena can be a bar as much as a debating chamber), the greater the danger that parliament will come to represent an additional, if not simply an enlarged bureaucracy.

Nevertheless, if only because time is always limited, resources strained, and a large assembly unwieldy—factors that are invariably under estimated by students of parliament from outside—the principle of collegiality has to be qualified in practice. Moreover, if they want genuinely to influence events in circumstances of advanced industrialised democracies, parliaments have to some extent

---

[61] See for example, Butt, *op. cit.*, pp. 251–74 and passim.

to order their work so that it is informed, rational, co-ordinated and practicable. Reconciling these ends with the fundamental principle of collegiality must, therefore, be a principal aim of the adaptation of parliamentary assemblies to modern conditions.[62]

The interdependence of different levels of government

There is even greater need to reconsider the traditional identification of parliaments with national self-determination, because the significance of national sovereignty is being eroded from two different directions with similar consequences. First, the historical function of parliament as a unifying force in nation building must be seen in relation to new demands for the devolution of government and political representation to lower levels. Most of the Member States of the European Community face the challenge of such demands, ranging in intensity from national separatism to calls for greater local autonomy within the existing State structure. Some of them already operate systems in which parliaments exist both at the level of national or federal government and at that of regional or state governement. Partly this internal stratification of political representation is an attempt to overcome some of the obstacles to parliamentary democracy, with its predilection for shared laws, common government and collegial authority. But parliamentary democracy and federalism seek similar ends and rely on each other to attain them.[63] The rigid association of parliaments with national sovereignty can, therefore, be self defeating, especially when the power of government itself extends below and above the national level.

The challenge to national sovereignty coming in the other direction, from international interdependence, is of course, of particular interest to this study. We have already seen in the last chapter how the development of the European Community itself should be seen as one way of responding to the threat to representative democracy of the exercise of political power across and above national boundaries. The European Parliament exists, I have been suggesting, for the very purpose of extending parliamentary democracy to compensate for the role that national parliaments can no longer play. Parliamentarism, therefore, acquires a supranational and a subnational dimension as the only way of responding to the growing interdependence of geographical levels of government. I shall deal in the last chapter with the relations between parliaments at different levels and how they should be approached in these circumstances, though the problems are considerable. The experience of federal systems suggests, however, that the adaptation can be made, while the failure of parliaments acting at a national level to counter the expansion of governments into subnational and supranational units, or to prevent the escape of political power in those directions, shows that it has to be attempted.

---

[62] I have drawn in this treatment of collegiality on Vile, *op. cit.*, pp. 337–42.
[63] For typically contrasting parliamentary reactions in Britain, see M. Rush and M. Shaw, *The House of Commons: Services and Facilities*, (London, 1974), pp. 242–68. On other countries, see Janet Morgan, *Reinforcing Parliament*, (London PEP, Vol. XLII Broadsheet No. 562, March 1976).

Conclusion

The main point of this chapter for the study as a whole is that the opportunity to make decisions about the future of the European Parliament should be used to re-think the role of parliament in general and to react to the crisis of parliamentary institutions in Europe in particular. It would be wrong to recommend procedural or organisational changes for the European Parliament based on the experience of parliaments elsewhere without first asking what those parliaments are basically for. There is no easy answer to that question either in political theory or in European experience.

The widespread sense that parliament is in decline is linked to fundamental developments in the nature of government itself and in the representative process. Attempts have been made to interpret the decline as a change in functions rather than as a loss of power, maintaining that formal, constitutional powers are less important in practice than parliament's ability to act as a channel of communication between people and government, a source of recruitment of political leaders, a check on administrative inefficiency and injustice, and generally as a secondary, but nevertheless useful, source of legitimacy for government in democratic regimes. While it is true, however, that many traditional ways of interpreting parliament's role are wrong, the functionalist approach gives neither an adequate account of the worries practitioners and academic specialists seem to have about parliament's present role, nor of the great diversity from one country to another and in different political circumstances, especially in the way formal powers are used. In fact, parliament is still far more than a mere instrument for providing legitimacy, though several trends in government and politics have tended to reduce it to that.

The same pressures and obstacles do not exist, however, at a European level, at least not yet and not to the same extent. That is partly because, as was shown in Chapter III, the European Community has not yet fully emerged as a body politic that can be compared to its Member States. Does this mean that the European Parliament should launch a renaissance of parliamentary democracy and in a way that parliaments in the Member States of the Community.acting individually could not? Before answering that question we have to understand the true nature of the decline of parliaments within the European nations.

I have suggested here that the decline should be seen essentially in terms of differences about the idea of parliamentary democracy itself, rather than as a change of functions or a loss of power. To a large extent alternative political ideas like popular democracy and corporatism have overshadowed that of parliamentary democracy and have produced circumstances unfavourable, to say the least, to its application in modern conditions of government. The idea of parliamentary democracy itself needs refinement, for example, in relation to the separation of powers, to the principle of collegiate authority and to the erosion of national sovereignty as a basis for self determination. I shall suggest in the concluding chapter ways in which the European Parliament can adapt the idea of parliamentary democracy in spite of these difficulties and I shall draw there on experience somewhat wider than that of the Member States of the Community.

Secondly, however, the way people view parliament is partly a consequence of

88

the existing balance of strength of political organisations. For parliament is used to gain access to government and its role will therefore depend in practice on the relations between the main political forces and how they see both the immediate and the ultimate aims of government. No assessment of the future possibilities of the European Parliament can be complete, therefore, unless it takes account of the nature of politics within the Community itself particularly the political choices at stake and the logistics available to political organisations. In the concluding chapter, therefore, I shall take up the threads of Chapter III and try to see what the relevant political circumstances of the directly elected European Parliament are likely to be.

Note to Chapter IV
This review of recent attitudes to parliamentary reform in some West European countries may serve to illustrate both the differences in national circumstances and the growing convergence towards a 'functional' view of parliament. But it is also intended to illustrate that the impression of a decline of parliament is not adequately explained by such a view.

British parliamentary reform
Since many continental reformers—and not only in recent years—have tended to treat the British parliamentary tradition as something of a model, it is especially important to begin by recognising just how far faith in that model has been eroded in Britain itself. Much of the disillusionment has come from realising the full implications of the traditional British model. As one practitioner recently stated:
> 'To put it baldly the government governs; Parliament is the forum where the exercise of government is publicly displayed and is open to scrutiny and criticism. And the Commons does not control the executive—not in any real sense; rather the executive controls the Commons through the exercise of their party majority power'.[1]

However, the purpose of most reform, proposed and actual, has been to make adaptations within that model. Although many of the recent arguments about the need for parliamentary reform are not at all new to the period since the second world war or even to this century, the question acquired its greatest practical significance for at least half a century when the Labour Government officially espoused a package of procedural and other changes in the period from 1966 to 1968. That period is known, after the Leader of the House of the Commons at the time, as the era of 'the Crossman reforms'. The package itself was intended essentially as a compromise. Although the views of more or less detached experts on parliament were obtained in a way that was unprecedently concerted and

---

[1] Michael Ryle, in S. A. Walkland and M. Ryle (eds.), *The Commons in the Seventies*, (London, 1977), pp. 12–13.

direct,[2] its object was primarily and not surprisingly political. The government was chiefly concerned about getting its programme of legislation through Parliament, although the general sense among political and constitutional observers of a decline of Parliament's power in relation to the executive was certainly taken into account. Indeed, ministers and senior officials were no doubt genuinely convinced that what they saw as the inefficiency of parliamentary procedure could not be cured simply by imposing further restrictions on debate. The threat of indiscipline within the Parliamentary Labour Party, however, was one factor and so was the fervour of many front and back bench members of both main parties to preserve the existing conventions.

An important new element, on the other hand, was a largely new group of mainly younger MPs seeking a professional career in politics but not expecting to obtain executive office at an early date.[3] This group of MPs shared with most academic reformers, and with a number of officers of Parliament, the view that substantial changes could and should be made which would give backbenchers a more constructive role and also provide greatly improved means for parliament to obtain and process information, as well as to publicise, criticise and influence government. There was a crucial vagueness about whether, or to what extent, backbenchers should actually obtain greater power in relation to the executive but it was generally agreed that: 'too much time is spent on ritualistic forms of debates and divisions on legislation which is going to be passed anyway. Too little time is spent on scrutiny of the administration.'[4] In other words, the functional view of parliament as 'a centre of political communication, and a two way process', held sway and it was generally assumed, at least overtly, that 'Parliament should not and does not threaten the ability of a government to govern'.[5] In fact, this last assumption provided an essential peg on which to hang the compromise. What the reformers demanded mainly was greater specialisation, better facilities for MPs, improved means of publicity and a more professional role for members. Their main proposal amounted to the establishment of a system of specialised select committees of backbenchers empowered to inquire into and report on the various continuing activities of government.[6]

It was only after hard bargaining with his ministerial colleagues that Crossman was able to offer some experimental steps in the direction pointed by the reformers. Rationalisation of parliamentary procedure and organisation was the

---

[2] Especially through the Study of Parliament Group, a small private association of academic specialists and officers of parliament. Some of the Group's members were privately consulted about the Labour Government's reforms, have given evidence to influential Select Committees on Procedure over a number of years and have both collectively and individually produced a number of influential writings on parliamentary reform. See, for example, A. H. Hanson and Bernard Crick, *The Commons in Transition*, (London, 1970).

[3] Much of this is confirmed in Crossman's own posthumous memoirs, *Diaries of a Cabinet Minister*, Volume II (London, 1976) *passim*.

[4] Bernard Crick, *The Reform of Parliament,* (London, 1964), p. 193.

[5] Bernard Crick, in Hanson and Crick, *op. cit.*, pp. 251 and 269.

[6] See Bernard Crick, *The Reform of Parliament, op. cit.*, pp. 198–200; The Study of Parliament Group, *Reforming the Commons*, (London, 1965).

predominant tone of the package, as it has continued to be in all British governments' schemes of parliamentary reform. The questions at issue, as stated by Crossman himself, were whether legislation was adopted at the 'speed required by the tempo of modern industrial change';whether there could be more time for topical debates and for 'political education' on the great issues and 'while accepting that legislation and administration must be firmly in the hands of the government, does the House of Commons provide a continuous and detailed check on the work of the executive and an effective defence of the individual against bureaucratic injustice and incompetence'?[7] The results included a streamlining of legislative and other procedure, improved pay and facilities for MPs, the establishment of the office of Parliamentary Commissioner for Administration, and an experiment with select committees of enquiry and report.

Only some of the select committees survived more than a few years and these have proved a small addition to those that already existed dealing with general subject areas rather than with particular government departments. The greatest disappointment has undoubtedly been over the relative failure of the experiment with select committees. This was because either the committees embarrassed the executive and were discontinued or disarmed, or they performed useful but unexciting work as 'a sideshow of no political importance'.[8] MPs were reluctant to serve on the committees and scarce resources were strained.[9] In retrospect, the most important component of the reform package was the easing of discipline within the Labour Party and the eventual advancement of some younger MPs to junior office. The effects of these changes greatly lessened the Government's need to consider further demands for parliamentary reform.[10]

Subsequently, a Conservative Government in 1971 went a good deal further with committees by establishing the Select Committee on Expenditure with specialised sub-committees dealing not only with financial but also general administrative aspects of the different sectors of government. The new Committee formed part of a general rationalisation of budgetary procedure in which publicity, deliberation and scrutiny of the broad expenditure decisions were emphasised instead of the annual procedures of formal approval of estimates. The work of the Expenditure Committee depended on the viability of a 'managerial' as opposed to a legislative approach to control of public expenditure and administration. However, the results in terms of real influence on government decisions have been disappointing.[11] The fundamental weakness of backbench

---

[7] Quoted by Crick in Hanson and Criek, *op. cit.*, p. 249.

[8] S. A. Walkland in Walkland and Ryle, *op. cit.*, p. 250.

[9] See Nevil Johnson, Select Committees as Tools of Parliamentary Reform, in Hanson and Crick, *op. cit.*, pp. 224–48; and Select Committees as Tools of Parliamentary Reform: Some Further Reflections, in Walkland and Ryle, *op. cit.*, pp. 175–201.

[10] See Crossman, *op. cit.*

[11] See S. A. Walkland, Parliamentary Control of Public Expenditure in Britain, in D. Coombes et al., *The Power of the Purse, op. cit.*, pp. 179–197; for the concept of a 'managerial' approach to budgetary control, see *ibid.* pp. 370, 376. On the role of Select Committee on Expenditure, see Ann Robinson, *Parliament and Public Spending*, (London, 1978).

committees remains the continued ability of the executive to draw their teeth when it wants. They cannot be assumed to 'have any specific effects on the roles of the main actors in the process of government'.[12] Nevertheless, there has been a recent revival in 1978 within the House itself of the idea of specialist committees of inquiry and it is probably true to say that the idea that backbenchers must be more than mere 'lobby-fodder' has now taken a grip that cannot be easily dislodged or prevented from making a significant change to the character of parliament.[13]

The real problem with attempts to extend specialised select committees in Britain has been that the proposal raised false expectations. It was supposed that a way could be found of genuinely redressing the balance of power in favour of backbenchers (which is what Crossman himself often professed to desire) without at the same time essentially disrupting the British model in which a majority committed to the programme of the executive could eventually get its way (to which Crossman and many of the reformers were also committed in practice).

The same ambivalence about the balance of power runs through most attempts to reform parliament in Britain. The fact is that reforms designed to enhance the role of parliament as a communicator, as a means of checking administration, and as a venue basically for support for and opposition to a government are by definition not designed to change the system of government. But it is precisely because they had some fundamental doubts about that system that some of the reformers sought change, while for backbenchers themselves it was invariably because they wanted a taste of real power. What has done immeasurably more than procedural reform to shake the foundations of executive domination and to alter long standing customs of British parliamentary life, has been the experience since 1974 of minority government and the growth in importance of minor parties in the House of Commons. New developments in British politics in the last five years have indeed brought the whole question of the role of parliamentary institutions, as well as other fundamental aspects of the British Constitution, more critically into focus than the reformers of the sixties could ever have imagined. Some of them have become much more bold and articulate in diagnosing the weaknesses of parliament and consequently now admit that the need for change lies not in adapting parliament to new functions but in questioning the basic conventions of the British model itself:

'What is needed if new ground now lost is to be regained is political realignment to the point where no government is in a position to act as the political arm of a powerful minority interest, whether to the Left or the Right, and where its main allegiance is of political necessity and considerations of survival to a broader-based and representative House of Commons. Change of this nature cannot come from Parliament itself—it must reflect new political and social impulses relayed through the structure of the national party system,

---

[12] Nevil Johnson in Hanson and Crick, *op. cit.*, p. 247.
[13] See First Report from the Select Committee on Procedure, Session 1977/78. Vol. I. HC 588–I (1977/78).

although much could be done to facilitate it through electoral reform. Procedural tinkering is in these circumstances irrelevant; the search for it dissipates energies which would be better employed in analysing the political problem.'[14]

I have dealt at some length with recent attitudes to reform in Britain because so many characteristics of the British model have attracted other countries in Western Europe. What they associate with Britain and even seek to import are qualities such as government stability and direct answerability of government to the electorate, a government's ability to uphold measures desired by a majority against parliamentary obstruction, and the way confrontation of Government and official Opposition supposedly clarifies the main political choices that the people themselves can then make in a general election. Ironically, just when in Britain the real benefits of these traits are being doubted, some continental European countries have been deliberately trying to copy them.

The French parliament

In France, the redefinition of parliament's role in the Constitution of the Fifth Republic and the no less important internal changes made in the rules of procedure of the National Assembly, were a conscious attempt to borrow the presumed advantages of the British model. The 'parlementarisme rationalisé' that has resulted was designed by placing constitutional limitations on both the scope and flexibility of parliament's legislative powers, by restricting the power to force governments to resign by motion of censure or interpellation, by severely limiting the role of specialised committees, by establishing executive control of parliament's agenda and rules of procedure, and above all by establishing in the Presidency of the Republic a new basis for executive authority which is constitutionally and practically separate from parliament.[15] But most commentators seem to agree that the most influential factor in changing the role of parliament was the introduction of direct election of the President of the Republic in 1962 and the dominant political role for most of the period since 1958 of the Gaullist party with a majority of seats in the Assembly. Even with the relative decline in the strength of the Gaullists since the death of President Pompidou, the cumulative and deliberate polarisation of politics was further marked during the Assembly elections in March 1978. Even if there is still no real diminution in the number of parties, polarised competition was increasingly being suggested as the norm.

In this sense it could be said that a major reform of parliament in France has already taken place. There is hardly any overt desire to return to the 'government by assembly' associated with the Third and Fourth Republics. It may sometimes be argued that the disembodiment of the Assembly brought about by the Fifth Republic has gone too far and has reduced respect for representative institutions

---

[14] Walkland in Walkland and Ryle, *op. cit.*, pp, 242–3. See also Stuart Walkland, The Politics of Parliamentary Reform, in John P. Mackintosh (ed.), *The People and Parliament* (London, 1978), pp. 184–97.
[15] See Philip Williams, *The French Parliament 1958/1967*, (London, 1968), pp. 11–23, 56–83.

to an extent that may be difficult to correct. However, as Avril has pointed out, on lines that fit closely the functionalist line of argument, it is profound social changes in France, as well as the constitutional measures themselves, that have forced parliament to adapt its role.[16] Deputies are persuaded to stop thinking in terms of a 'golden age' of parliamentary republicanism in which each individual deputy acted himself as an agent for converting demands into policies, and governments had continually to convince a majority that was not assured in advance. In its new role parliament is no longer a transformer but a transmitter, a relay station between people and government.[17]

Parliament is no less seen as an essential part of the regime in this role. In particular, there has been much criticism of the extent to which the majority dominates the Assembly, depriving the opposition of means of challenging, ventilating, criticising and checking the government. Reforms have been pressed and some have been made to reinforce parliament's functions as 'a tribune where needs and demands are publicly formulated and their different aspects illuminated in the course of a polarised debate' and 'where all the great national issues find expression'.[18] To the same end and to enhance also parliament's functions of political education and publicity, there have been steps to provide better means for discussion of topical issues, to develop the investigatory role of committees particularly by public hearings, to increase public interest by televising parliament and to strengthen the services and facilities of parliament, not only for assisting its own members but also for informing the general public about its proceedings. As the collective role of parliament has declined in importance, so the role of the individual deputy as a kind of 'welfare officer' has increased mediating directly between his constituents and the State.[19]

It is difficult to see, on the other hand, how certain worries that are sometimes expressed about the way the Republic is governed can be quietened simply by facilitating parliament's functions of communication and administrative scrutiny. There has been considerable debate, for example, about what would happen if the majority in the Assembly was composed in such a way as to be consistently opposed to the President of the Republic. In such circumstances the government would presumably come to depend again on the Assembly rather than on the President on a strict interpretation of the Constitution.[20] The spectre of a recalcitrant, obstructive and interventionist Assembly, in which power was effectively dispersed among different individuals and groups, may not be laid for good. An Assembly majority opposed to the President of the Republic is not likely to be satisfied with improved means of ventilating grievances, debating major issues and investigating specialised aspects of administration.

Moreover a feature that is increasingly common to liberal democratic regimes, but seems to have been discussed most prominently in France, is what is known

---

[16] Pierre Avril, *Les Français et leur Parlement*, (Paris, 1972), passim but especially pp. 59–67.

[17] *Ibid.*, p. 65. The general preference of 'executive-dominated' government can perhaps be sensed in the opposition parties' resistance to the reforms of parliament proposed by President Giscard.

[18] Maurice Duverger, *La Monarchie Républicaine*, (Paris, 1974), p. 183.

[19] See *Ibid.*, pp. 184–5: Avril & Feydy, in European Parliament, *op. cit.*, p. 17.

[20] See Maurice Duverger, *Echec au Roi*, (Paris, 1978).

as the 'personalisation of power'. The personal role of the President of the Republic has been limited even since 1962, if mainly in domestic matters, by the need for the executive to take account of the views of the majority in the Assembly. (Even in the heyday of the Gaullist party, the Assembly was far from monolithic and succeeded not only in influencing the choice of Prime Minister but also in amending legislation and the budget.) Especially since 1974 a form of 'personal government' has been emerging, however, in which the President increasingly governs through his prime minister and cabinet.[21] The long term prospects of a system of government based on polarised opinions and personalised leadership have led some to recommend that the role of deputies as political intermediaries should be restored. Many wonder whether parliamentary politics ought not to be revived to increase the supply of political figures with the authority and ability to challenge the bureaucracy and to bring greater dynamism into government.[22] The parliamentary mandate would have to carry more prospect of real influence and control, if that were to happen, especially if it is to continue to hold out little promise as a path to executive office.[23] The 'atomised' character of French political life, so long recognised as a fundamental problem, is not altered by parliament's decline as a focus of special interests, or by the executive's monopoly of formulating and expressing the general interest.[24] In the absence of an effective national forum for processing their different interests and demands, the divided elements of the country tend to seek alternative means of expression.

The parliament of the German Federal Republic
The British model has also influenced the role of parliament in the German Federal Republic. Other influences have been just as important, however, including the United States, but particularly the rich and diverse experience of parliamentary government both at national and state level in Germany itself especially during the nineteenth century. This indigenous experience of parliamentarism in Germany has been sadly overlooked by foreign students, since it presents some distinctive traits that do much to determine contemporary procedure and behaviour (and have also been very influential in the European Parliament, as we have seen).

Again, the method by which parliamentary government was established in the Federal Republic represented in itself a kind of reform, given that an overriding aim was to avoid the sort of role that parliament had played previously in the

---

[21] *Ibid.*, p. 176 ff. On the 'personalisation of power' as a trend in liberal democracies generally, and not only in France, see Roger-Gérard Schwarzenberg, *L'État Spectacle: Essai sur et contre le Star System en Politique*, (Paris, 1977).

[22] Duverger, 1978, pp. 403–4, Stanley Hoffman, *Sur la France*, Paris, Seuil, 1976, p. 289; Williams, *op. cit.*, p. 117, Avril, *op. cit.*, p. 72.

[23] See Avril, *op. cit.*, pp. 137–40.

[24] *Ibid.*, pp. 131–45. See also, Hoffmann, pp. 225–90.

Weimar Republic.[25] A deliberate attempt was made in effect to move away from a traditional idea in Germany of parliament as an institution essentially of opposition, in which each deputy and each party acted as the spokesman of some particular regional or other interest. In the new constitutional arrangements there are various provisions designed to avoid the instability and the diffused power of the *Parteienstaat* which had dominated Weimar and was held responsible for the eventual downfall of parliamentary government altogether.

Thus the Basic Law contains provisions to protect the executive against the effects of party instability and to discourage the multiplication of small parties and factions. Although the Chancellor as head of the government is elected by the Bundestag, there is a separation of powers between parliament and the executive and the Bundestag is able to dismiss the Chancellor only if it is able at the same time to name his successor. This has meant, in practice, that cabinets normally last for the fixed term of four years—the power of appointment passing in practice to the electorate or at least to the political parties. Indeed, although most governments in the Republic have been coalitions, polarisation between two dominant, major parties has clearly emerged, with the role of the Bundestag being determined largely by the fact that deputies align themselves in terms of a majority and an opposition. Again, it has been the development of such a stable party system rather than constitutional provisions alone that has determined the main features.[26]

The result is now widely recognised abroad as the leading example in Western Europe of a parliamentary system effectively combining responsiveness with responsible government. Indeed, it seems that the Federal Republic may be replacing Britain as the model of modern parliamentary government. One special reason for that, however, and a feature of the Bundestag's role which distinguishes it sharply both from the British House of Commons and the French National Assembly is that it is predominantly a legislative institution. It is, moreover, one in which individual deputies and groups of deputies can have an effective influence on federal legislation and on federal government expenditure. The key to the Bundestag's legislative role is its organisation into specialised committees which examine and report on bills before they go to the chamber as a whole. Although the initiative in law making rests in practice overwhelmingly with the executive, parliamentary committees play a substantial part in amending legislation. The executive will usually get its way in general matters, if it is determined, but 'there is always uncertainty in the legislative process' and proposals have to be 'negotiated rather than imposed'.[27] This means among other

---

[25] See Peter H. Merkl, Party Government in the Bonn Republic, in Elka Frank (ed.), *Lawmakers in the Modern World*, *op. cit.*, pp. 65–82; G. Loewenberg, *Parliament in the German Political System*, (Ithaca, N.Y., 1966). Other influences were no less important from the British one, however, including not only that of the USA, but also the rich and diverse experience of parliamentary government at national and state level within Germany itself in the nineteenth century.

[26] Merkl, *op. cit.*; Loewenberg, *op. cit.*; Kurt Sontheimer, *The Government and Politics of West Germany*, (London, 1972), pp. 11–39, 116–22.

[27] Nevil Johnson, *Government in the Federal Republic of Germany*, (Oxford, 1973), p. 86. See also, Loewenberg, *op. cit.*, p. 430.

things that the federal administration, including its senior officials, has to take a real and continuing interest in the political game as it is played out in parliament: officials are usually responsible for defending measures personally before Bundestag committees and even for negotiating settlements. The public administration is therefore exposed to politics in a way that it is not at all in Britain and France.

Nevertheless, fundamental problems in the working of parliamentary institutions have been evident in studies of the Federal Republic as they have been elsewhere in Western Europe. The theme of personalisation of power is present, though to a much lesser degree than when the ironical description of 'Chancellor Democracy' was applied to the system under Adenauer's Chancellorship, and seems to be checked by the relative independence of the Bundestag, the selection of ministers predominantly with parliamentary experience and the existence of supplementary centres of power in the states of the federation. More serious has been the fear that the very stability of the system, the exclusiveness induced by the dominance of the two major parties and their tendency to compete for the middle ground will produce a narrow governing consensus, lower confidence in the reality of political competition, and encourage extra-parliamentary opposition.

In this respect, however, the sense of potential crisis is much less than during the years of the Grand Coalition between 1968 and 1970. What critics of parliament regret above all are its detachment from the people, its weakness in ventilating the 'great issues' and holding genuine public confrontations of different views of government and society.[28] It seems, indeed, that the very 'workmanlike' character of an assembly in which specialised, legislative activity is at a premium and where the professional career politician predominates, extracts a high cost in public awareness and access. It does not, after all, seem to place parliament any higher in public esteem, and may diminish public interest and weaken the general public's sense of real participation. In his major study of the German parliament Loewenberg concludes that it is the particular achievements of the Federal Republic rather than the role of parliament itself that account for the apparent legitimacy of the new regime of parliamentary democracy.[29]

Indeed, it is the remoteness of the Bundestag and its introversion, which have worried reformers most. When it has not been concerned mainly with improving the services and facilities of members, especially through the political party secretariats, or with improving the committee system, parliamentary reform has sought to increase opportunities both for topical public debate and for airing matters of direct concern to the individual citizens.[30] In the early 1960s a Question Hour was established, and subsequently there has been provision for short debates on topical issues (*Aktuelle Stunde*) and for wider use of interpella-

---

    [28] Loewenberg, *op. cit.*, pp. 393 ff.; Sontheimer, p. 132.
    [29] Loewenberg, *op. cit.*, pp. 429–30.
    [30] See Uwe Thaysen's contribution to European Parliament, *op. cit.*, pp. 49–60. See also U. Thaysen, *Parlamentsreform in Theorie und Praxis*, (Opladen, 1972).

tions in written form to obtain information on specific matters. Members still show a relative lack of interest in opportunities for general debate, however, and it is still in committees (and normally in private) that much politically important activity takes place. Committees of investigation have not proved successful on those occasions when they have been used, though there is a growing interest in public hearings by specialist committees. Televising of proceedings, outside the major political debates, seems to have struck the public most by revealing the number of empty seats in the chamber. As Sontheimer suggests, the real problem with parliamentary reform up to now could be the lack of an articulate, common view of what the role of parliament should be, an uncertainty that seems to affect also the general public image of the institution in West Germany.[31]

Parliaments in smaller European States

The post-war experience of the smaller States of Western Europe, however, illustrates that a stable executive can be combined with parliamentary government without a polarisation of electoral or parliamentary politics. It also shows, however, that the apparent decline of parliament as a national centre of political life, and its low standing in public esteem, are felt even where many political parties compete on more or less equal terms for electoral support, and where governments depend for survival on the support of a number of different parliamentary groups. Smallness in population and area, and accurate proportionality in the distribution of seats in parliament according to the electoral support for the various parties, do not seem to prevent a dislocation, even a sense of competing authority, between people and parliament.

In some of the smaller parliamentary democracies, stability has normally been achieved because the major parties (anything from three to five in number) have made the necessary arrangements among themselves for the creation and maintenance of governments. That usually means fixing the main lines of legislation and policy in advance as a basis of any agreed coalition. Moreover, in coalition-forming, the role of parliament itself may not be directly important. There may be a deep commitment to compromise among the leaders of the main parties and a common understanding that the distinct components of the society which they claim to represent must be included in any governing arrangement. There can also be a tendency for parties to be closely tied with religious, social and economic interests that are more powerful influences on government than parliament acting alone or independently.

In the Low Countries, for example, although at least for the last hundred years parliamentary support has been considered necessary for the survival of a government, it is the executive that governs and individual MPs are closely tied to their particular party organisation and the social and political 'family' that it represents.

Nevertheless, there have been signs of a decline of confidence in the traditional governing compromise and sometimes also in the traditional parties (many of them confessional) on which it is founded. In the Netherlands there have been

---

[31] Sontheimer, *op. cit.*, p. 134.

demands—leading to the emergence of new minority political parties—for constitutional changes to bring the people directly into the process of forming governments and into the basic choices from which legislation and policy flow. There are signs there of a conscious polarisation as well as party competition based on political differences, rather than party compromise based on an understanding among social and religious groups. Some discern a trend (especially with the relative decline of confessional parties) towards a confrontation of government and opposition somewhat on British and West German lines.[32]

In the Scandinavian countries, however, while the same sort of factors as elsewhere have limited parliament's role as a legislature and in controlling the executive, its role as an elective body has certainly survived. At the same time, parliament's active function of legitimation of government has not removed criticisms of remoteness, or the threat of conflict between people and parliament. This has been illustrated in Denmark by the appearance in parliament of new protest parties as well as by increasing recourse to referenda which tend to produce results different from those reflected in parliament itself on the same questions, and can be found in demands for greater internal party democracy and for extra-parliamentary forms of public, 'grass-roots' participation in government. As in all the smaller countries, parliamentary reform has been an issue but on familiar lines of rationalising procedure, providing for greater professionalism and specialisation, and seeking to increase discussion of topical and popular issues and public information about parliament.[33] That type of reform or the genuine dependence of the executive on parliamentary support do not seem, however, to alter the underlying scepticism among the general public about the power of parliament.

Parliamentary reform in Italy
In post-war Italy, on the other hand, the dependence of governments on parliamentary support is often widely and directly associated with the regime's shortcomings: in this case the instability and immobility of 'government by assembly'. Nevertheless, as elsewhere, it is not in fact parliament itself, but the political parties—and particularly the majority Christian Democracy—that are seen as responsible for appointing governments and cabinet instability results mainly from internal divisions within the cabinet as well as within the majority party.[34] Indeed, votes of confidence are used by cabinets to discourage parliamentary obstruction by backbench deputies of the majority.

The overriding complaint about the role of parliament in the Italian Republic, in fact, has been less its exercise of elective powers than its use of legislative powers.

---

[32] See Jan Kooiman's contribution to European Parliament, *op. cit.*, pp. 133–56. In Belgium on the other hand, new minority parties have also emerged but the new divisions concern the very structure of the state.

[33] See Erik Damgaard's contribution to European Parliament, pp. 34–48. Similar reforms have been canvassed in the Belgian and Dutch parliaments, see J. Gérard-Libois, *ibid.*, pp. 29–38, and Kooiman, *ibid.*, pp. 133–56.

[34] P. A. Allum, *Italy: Republic without Government?*, (London, 1973), pp. 66–93.

Italy provides another example of a parliament which acts as a legislature, and which at the same time enjoys substantial independence of the executive in organising its own time table and procedures. As in West Germany specialised legislative committees are the main theatre of parliamentary activity. Indeed, these committees actually pass about three-quarters of the total number of laws made by parliament in Italy, a total that is itself vast (about 220 a year) and includes a substantial proportion (30 per cent) introduced by individual back-bench deputies. Although government sponsored bills have the greatest chance of success, even they are normally subject to substantial amendment arising from counter proposals in parliament. Recent research by Predieri, however, has shown how the legislative proposals with which parliament deals consist predominantly of *'leggine'*, that is, minor bills dealing with 'micro-sectional' questions.[35] In fact, parliament's legislative activity has increasingly become a process in which regional, social and economic interests seek to obtain measures to their advantage, using the members of specialised committees as their intermediaries.[36] The main criticisms are that most of the legislation deals with detailed matters that should be the business of the administration rather than parliament and that the plethora of new laws that results makes little or no difference to the basic immobility of the administration, tied up as it is in a network of existing legal restrictions, often dating from the time of Mussolini and before. What parliament should be doing, it is claimed, is seeking to bring coherence and order into the existing legal framework. As Predieri puts it: 'parliament is criticised not because it produces many minor detailed laws but because it fails to bring out major laws'.[37]

Most proposals, and actual measures, of reform have sought to increase the efficiency of the legislative process, while improving the means by which parliament can act as a channel of communication between people and government. However, there have been sustained demands for further reform and many deputies especially in the Communist Party seek greater power to influence government. Increasingly since 'the opening to the left' over a decade ago, parliament has been seen as a means of including the Communists in power without giving them the responsibility of government. One trend, therefore, is to envisage a kind of division of functions between executive and parliament, in which the former is entrusted with general strategy and the basic principles of government policy, while parliament acts mainly to articulate and co-ordinate interests and to control the administration. Rationalisation of procedure has been proposed by supporters of the majority, for example, to include greater legislative delegation to the executive, greater acceptance of executive initiative in law making, and subordinating parliament's own legislative activity to a government programme. In return it is suggested that parliament can be given

---

[35] See Alberto Predieri, Parlamento 1975, in Predieri (ed.), *Il Parlamento nel Sistema Politico Italiano*, (Milan, 1975), pp. 11–93.

[36] Andrea Manzella, *Il Parlamento*, (Bologna, 1977), pp. 81–100.

[37] Predieri's contribution to European Parliament, *op. cit.*, pp. 200–1.

greater opportunities for expressing opposition, even for taking its own initiatives, by measures which do not threaten the government's general programme, and policies and, above all, do not threaten its survival.[38]

In particular, there has been intensive discussion and some actual innovation of procedures (especially in the reforms to the Chamber's rules of procedure made in 1971) designed to develop parliament's means of obtaining information about, and reporting on, the activities of government, or *L'ispezione* as it has become generally known.[39] One important innovation has been the right of a committee to pass resolutions within its field of competence and to follow up the results of a previous inquiry. In fact parliament may use powers of inquiry not only by setting up special committees of inquiry (a means limited by the need for majority approval in the Chamber) but also through the use of 'watchdog' committees, and by considering reports from government departments, public agencies and the Corte dei Conti. For some years now, the specialised legislative committees have been making increasing use of hearings. To the existing widely used procedures of questions and interpellations has now been added the right of a committee to request information on particular matters from a minister or his department, or from agencies under his tutelage. These opportunities can be used not only to obtain and publicise information but also to criticise the administration, and even to bring parliament into the decision making process of government itself, for example, by following up an inquiry with political pressure including votes in parliament.[40] The assumption behind most of these reforms is that there are areas where individual members of the majority and those of the opposition parties have interests in common and should be allowed to work together, as long as the fundamental decision of who governs is accepted.[41]

It cannot be said, therefore, that parliament in Italy is now purely an instrument of legitimation or of mobilising consent for government. It plays an important role as an arbitrator among special interests in its law making activities and is seen by the Communists at least as a means of exercising real influence and control over the activities of government.

Three questions in particular, however, are being disputed among would-be reformers. The first concerns the real purpose of *L'ispezione*: is it simply to obtain information and report, or is it to exercise some control of the public administration (and thereby of public policy) that is independent of the government of the day? Secondly, if the latter, can this really be seen as an appropriate activity for a parliamentary assembly, and can it be justified when the real problem in Italian government is not the absence of parliamentary intervention, but the distance that exists between the administration, on the one hand, and

[38] See Vincenzo Spaziante, Il Controllo Parlamentare: Quadro Politico e Orientamento Della Piu Recente Dottrina, in Prediere (ed.), *op. cit.*, pp. 251–72.

[39] See F. Cosentino, Regolamento della Camera e prassi parlamentare, in G. Amato (ed.), *L'indirizzo politico nel nuovo regolamento della Camera dei Deputati*, (Milan, 1969), pp. 55 ff.; G. Amato, *L'Ispezione politica del Parlamento*, (Milan, 1968).

[40] Manzella, *op. cit.*, pp. 123–72.

[41] Spaziante, *op. cit.*, pp. 267–9.

political direction on the other. Parliamentary control of the developed kind some deputies have been demanding can be defended as a means of backing up or supplementing ministers' own attempts to direct and control the public administration.

The third question to ask is, if parliament is to share in the function of *indirizzo politico*, on the basis of what sort of internal leadership and power structure is it to do so? It is to be at the cost of continued or even greater instability of governments, or on the basis of a deal between Christian Democracy and the Communists excluding the smaller parties, or even by accepting greater rationalisation of procedure in the ruling party's interests, in return for what are in effect superficial gains of better access to information that cannot then be used to influence events?[42]

---

[42] These and other arguments are debated at length in Predieri (ed.), *op. cit.*, and Amato (ed.), *op. cit.*

V   Towards a New Model Parliament

Why the future of the European Parliament matters

Two main conclusions have so far emerged from this study. First, that the European Community can achieve its main objectives and respect its basic principles only by developing into a democratic body politic. Second, that there is only a limited amount we can learn from experience within the Member States of the Community for creating such a body politic on principles of parliamentary democracy, given the untypical nature of the Community as a political entity and given also that parliamentary democracy is more comprehensible as a set of ideas than as a record of practice.

For two particular reasons these conclusions are of immediate importance for the European Parliament. First, as I tried to show in Chapter III, the Community's need for democratic political institutions does not arise only from some future objective, such as European Union, or from the introduction of direct elections but from the nature of the Community as it is now—its social and economic principles and aims, its body of law and procedure, the present role of its Institutions. The question of the European Parliament's future should not therefore be postponed on the grounds that it is really a subject for discussions about a different, more integrated type of Community. On the contrary, the need for democracy and above all the role of the Parliament itself should be tackled prior even to discussing new economic or political goals. In other words, since it is basic to the principles and aims of the Community that it exists to preserve and develop democratic institutions, a reform of the Community Institutions is overdue, especially in view of the need for vital decisions about the future economic policies of the Community and about admitting new Member States.

Secondly, the directly elected Parliament could take the opportunity to rethink the role of parliamentary institutions and to seek to develop at European level a form of parliamentary government that improves on what we have at national level. In fact, many of the constraints on parliamentary reform at national level do not apply in the Community although the circumstances at European level impose other sorts of constraint. It does suggest, however, that in borrowing from past experience the European Parliament should look more widely than parliamentary life within the Member States themselves. One reason for doing so is that it can hardly be said that parliamentary government has developed with particular effectiveness in the States of the Community. It is at least possible both that the experience from elsewhere, particularly the USA, might be more encouraging and that there will be greater chance of reaching the ideals of parliamentary democracy at European than there has been at State level.

Whether the European Parliament itself takes a similar view will depend partly, however, on the attitude of its own members, which in turn will be influenced by who they are, how they get into the Parliament, what various ties and loyalties they have, how they organise themselves and so on. We need, therefore, two perspectives on the future. To borrow from the jargon of social scientists who study the future methodically, we need an 'exploratory scenario' and an 'anticipatory scenario'. The first, which will concern mainly the sort of political circumstances in which the Parliament is likely to find itself following the first direct election, is intended to describe variations on the present caused by changes in relevant 'parameters'. The second, which will deal largely with the need for parliamentary democracy itself and what it means in terms of constitutional ground rules, attempts to portray a desired image of the future in terms of objectives or ideal standards.[1]

It should not be thought, however, that by distinguishing in this way between different perspectives on the future I am suggesting a distinction between a short and a long term. The distinction is rather one between prediction and prescription: what is prescribed is no less necessary (or more likely) in the immediate future than what is predicted. After this consideration of the future in general terms (summarising on the way the argument of earlier chapters), I shall turn to consider some of the main options facing the European Parliament in terms of specific aspects of its powers and organisations after direct election. That will take the form largely of an agenda for future research and debate by the Parliament itself.

The impact of direct election and the role of political parties

To picture the political circumstances of the directly elected Parliament, three 'parameters' are relevant: the Community framework itself, meaning the institutional powers and arrangements provided by the present corpus of Community law; the role of the governments of the Member States; and the role of political forces, either newly released on to the Community stage, or strengthened in their impact, as a result of direct elections. Only the last two offer much prospect of change.

I have explained in Chapter III why the Community framework has largely ceased to be, on its own, an effective source of political changes. Recent moves to set new goals for the Community have happened because the States' governments have acted, largely through the extra constitutional machinery of the 'European Council'. The most recent and typical example was the decision on a European Monetary System (EMS), where the Commission played a prominent

---

[1] Peter Hall (ed.) *Europe 2000* (London 1974) pp. 6–8.

part in the formative stages but inter-governmental diplomacy was the predominant method. However, although initiatives of that type are not to be excluded on substantive matters like EMS, the governments acting collectively are not likely to propose, let alone accept, the sort of institutional developments that were considered in Chapter III. There might be more scope, however, if we consider how they would react individually to initiatives taken elsewhere, or how shifting coalitions of governments might react, even on substantive issues, in a way that effectively led to political, and even ultimately constitutional, change. That could be important, since the support of the governments and even their concurrence in the taking of initiatives will continue to be essential for such change to occur.

What, therefore, are the prospects that out of the European Parliament there could arise some effective pressure for change in the methods by which the Community now operates? We have seen in Chapter II that with its present powers, composition and organisation, the Parliament has not succeeded in influencing the Community's development more than marginally. Even the introduction of direct elections is of limited significance without clearer definition of the Parliament's role. The qualified form of the first direct election was described in Chapter II. Are there any general consequences for the attitudes and behaviour of the Parliament's members that we can predict in view of the introduction of direct elections?

Direct elections are not likely, at least at first, to produce in the Parliament a clearly defined political grouping with an absolute majority. A majority grouping might emerge eventually following the forming of coalitions and alliances but it would still be unlikely for some time to share the same organisation at least for electoral purposes. In any event, after the first election, whatever the exact distribution of seats among different political groups (and however it compares with the present distribution), there will undoubtedly be many actual or potential political alliances. It is probably safe to assume, therefore, that the political complexion of the directly elected Parliament will be for the foreseeable future very similar to what it is now. However, the official political groups of the European Parliament, which play such an important role in its procedure and organisation, may well find it even more difficult to obtain discipline from their members and so may lose some of their authority. These groups do not anyway constitute political parties, mainly because they lack organisational means of fighting and winning elections. In spite of the formation of some European party federations, none of the successful candidates will have owed their success to a European political group.[2] Indeed, given the way the electoral procedure has been determined for the first election, party organisations in the States are likely, in the beginning at least, to be even more important in many respects in selecting candidates, ensuring their election, and influencing their subsequent behaviour,

<hr>

[2] On European party federations based on the Parliament's political groups, (so far christian, socialist and liberal) see John Fitzmaurice, *The European Parliament*, (London 1978), pp. 97–119; G. & P. Pridhams' contribution to S. Henig (ed.) *European Political Parties*, (London 1978). Both in States using a national list system of election and others the role of national party organisations may be expected to increase in importance compared with that of parliamentary parties.

than they have been up to now. Indeed, if it is right to assume that in general there will be a wider range of significant influence on the attitudes and behaviour of members, there will probably also be a larger number of non-aligned, or less potentially alignable, members than before. Three influences in particular can be expected to work against group formation and cohesion to a degree they have not up to now.

First, a number of members will be influenced primarily by loyalty to regional or local constituency interests. These interests in many respects will cut across State differences, and in some respects will underpin them. They can be expected to be significant not only in those States where regional or local constituencies have been defined but also where individual candidates can rely on local or regional support to improve their placing on national lists. Secondly, that same factor of individual position where national lists are used and the general problem that the campaigns of individual candidates will be more difficult to organise, even with the help of State parties, than in other types of election, will undoubtedly increase the dependence of many candidates on the support of organised interests and pressure groups. Thirdly, but chiefly in Denmark, France and Britain, we can expect the return of a number of candidates who will regard both their selection and election as committing them to a stance of outright opposition to the future development of the Community in anything other than the direction of a more inter-governmental arrangement, for which the establishment of European political parties, let alone a European body politic, is seen by them as both unnecessary and undesirable.

A European party system, therefore, is still something very much for the future. It is not even certain that the present political groups in the Parliament will form the basis of future European political parties. Whether such parties do emerge at all will depend among other things on whether a uniform electoral procedure is eventually introduced, but it probably depends most on whether a system of responsible government is established at a Community level. Indeed, it is less the result of the first direct election than the subsequent role of political organisations within the Parliament that is likely to determine the consequences for the Parliament itself. From what we know of the history of free elections, it would be extremely unusual if the election threw up of its own accord new political parties that could subsequently determine the Parliament's role.[3] It will

[3] On the factors determining the formation of political parties and definitions of the same, see especially G. Sartori, *Parties and party systems*, Vol. I (Cambridge 1976), pp. 3–29, 36–57, and S. M. Lipset and S. Rokkan *Party Systems and Voter Alignments: cross-national perspectives* (New York 1967), pp. 2–50. Comparative and theoretical studies of political parties have not so far taken account of the peculiar circumstances of the European Community. While in certain respects comparisons to less-developed countries can be made, they fall down in the sense that both the electorate and existing political parties in Western Europe are those of a developed system. It seems appropriate therefore to regard political parties (on Sartori's 'minimal' definition, p. 64) as existing so far only at a State level in the Community. I have retained, therefore, the official designation 'political groups' to describe the existing political organisations in the European Parliament and their successors after direct election. However, I have extended the historical use of the term 'faction' (in spite of Sartori's doubts) to describe the alliances and coalitions that might form in the Parliament in the near future across political groups. Shared political attitudes (for example on a left/right spectrum) I describe as 'tendencies'.

106

no doubt weaken some existing organisations, strengthen others and alter the circumstances in which new ones may form and old ones re-form. It may, as I have suggested, cause what the Parliament already has in the way of political organisation to be weaker. Indeed, some observers are inclined to see the holding of direct elections as a major risk for these reasons.[4]

On the other hand, the uncertainties regarding the role of political parties in the European Parliament at least mean that the choices about its future role are less restricted than they are for national parliaments. I shall deal with some of the choices themselves in later sections but they will not be realistic unless they take account of the political elements that will make up Parliament's membership after direct elections. No less than seven such elements seem at this stage to be likely to be significant, though their relative weight cannot be predicted.

(a) The official political groups that exist in the Parliament now, four of which are founded on so-called political 'families' (christian, liberal, socialist and communist), and two on associations of purely national parties (largely Conservatives, Gaullists and Irish Fianna Fail) which are likely to have significant membership in the new Parliament.

(b) Political tendencies viewed on a right/left spectrum largely of social and economic philosophy (neo-liberalism versus state intervention and so on); these tendencies to some extent divide the christian and liberal political 'families', cut across some political groups and are themselves divided both on general issues (such as supranationalism and the role of the Parliament itself) and on particular issues (such as reform of the common agricultural policy and enlargement).

(c) State interests, which may well be strengthened as a factor, not only among British, Danish and French members as a defence of States' rights against supranationalism but also among British, Irish and Italian members as part of a division between 'rich' and 'poor' States on issues like the future of EMS and enlargement of the Community, with new and possibly sinister meaning for the continuing solidarity of the Community itself.

(d) Other special interests on a regional and local basis, or a social and economic one, or both, which could well produce new loosely associated political groups or at least factions based on nationalist, regionalist or linguistic parties in Belgium, Italy and Britain but which will for the most part cut across official political groups.

(e) The Commission as a focus of support and opposition in relation to a defined programme or strategy.

(f) Individual State governments or coalitions of governments forming alliances with unofficial or official groups of members in the Parliament; a

---

[4] For a treatment of these arguments see Michael Steed, *The integration of national parties*, Paper delivered to the XIIth. Congress of the International Political Science Association at Edinburgh, August 16–21, 1976; and *The institutional framework of integration in Western Europe: the role of political parties*, Paper delivered to the Euro-Arab Conference at the European University Institute, Florence, May 1978.

h

factor limited both by fear of giving the Parliament greater influence and by the fact that the political complexion and attitude of governments fluctuates according to electoral and other changes at State level.

(g) The need for coalitions and alliances within the Parliament for electing its own President, Bureau and committee officers and members, and for determining its general procedures and strategies.

What are the prospects of these several elements being welded somehow into consistent and articulate political groupings, if not full political parties? Questions of parliamentary tactics could well take precedence over those of ideology and interest, in producing effective alignments. In other words, the last three elements identified here could in practice override the others. If they do so, it will be because, as I have argued in Chapter III, the substantive issues of Community politics turn out to be essentially questions of what sort of Community is to be desired and by what methods it is to be established. Such a conjecture seems plausible if we realise that the immediate general issues that the Community is likely to have to decide depend, when reduced to their particulars, on decisions about the allocation of resources. This can be said certainly of the question for the economic aims and principles of the Community and bcth also are linked to such continuing 'sectoral' questions as reform of the common agricultural policy and the development of regional policy. In other words, if they are to be effectively influenced by members of the Parliament, it must ultimately be by the Parliament having a much greater say in the role of the Community in economic policy and in decisions with budgetary implications.

All we can safely say at this stage, however, is that, whatever attitudes members take up, on substantive or constitutional issues, they will be able to press them effectively only by organising to use the Parliament's powers and procedures and ultimately by a further appeal to the electorate. That practical imperative must lead them to consider what role they want the Parliament to perform and why. In turn, therefore, they will need to take a view of the purposes of the Community itself, and implicitly of the sort of political entity it should be.

The question of Europe: what kind of polity?
There are senses in which it can be unhelpful to view the future in terms of a desired image or set of objectives: the result may cause conflict over principles that turn out not to be important in practice and it may also cause decisions to be postponed on the grounds that an image of the future is not attainable in the present. Defining ideal constitutional arrangements of a Community of the future has these disadvantages as was suggested in Chapter III. It is better, therefore, to think in terms of the general standards that should be applied in any further institutional development, standards that are as relevant and necessary now as they would be in any future rearrangement.

What is more, however, a purely academic or legal construction is of limited value compared with genuine political debate and resolution. Objective men, however wise, cannot be a substitute for the role of political forces and tendencies in settling such questions as what sort of Community should be sought and by what means. That is why those questions should be confronted by the directly elected Parliament. The sort of analysis offered here, however, has tried to help in three ways: by noting the ground rules suggested by practical needs and by the aims and principles accepted so far; by purifying the use of terms to limit misunderstanding and save effort; and by suggesting comparisons with past experience, not only in Europe, that might be instructive.

Agreement about the ground rules would be much easier if we could be more articulate and precise about three critical aspects of the Community's constitutional development so far: the relevance of federalism; the nature of a Community government; and the needs of a European body politic. If some consensus could be arrived at on these three aspects, it may not be necessary to do more than to build on the existing constitutional framework of the Community treaties. That framework has one outstanding advantage in being based on acceptance of the rule of law: that is no mean achievement as an advance beyond normal international relations. We have seen in this study that in many respects the limitations of the Community framework have become increasingly obvious beyond the specific provisions of the treaties for establishing the Common Market. If, however, the Member States are to continue to use the Community framework for making and implementing common policy, we cannot simply ignore the consequences for national sovereignty. The more that vital domestic political issues need to be settled in the framework of the Community, the more new methods must be found of binding people to their government. That requires laying down conditions for the exercise of government through the Community. In other words, we need to move from the idea of sovereignty as absolute power to that of sovereignty as power exercised subject to fixed conditions. The principle of constitutional government is, after all, essential to the compact on which the Community is based.

It is expressed above all in those features of the Community that may be described as federalist, not in the distorted view of federalism as cumulative and even unlimited integration but as a method of organising the relations between states on a constitutional basis. What can be misleading is that a great variety of regimes claim to be federal, some of which have long since abandoned the conditions of genuine federalism. What we need to do is to select from the idea of federalism what appears to be suitable from considerations of both practice and principle. Four essential conditions for a ground rule of Community federalism can be suggested therefore: the existence of political authority exercised separately from the Member States; the circumscription of that authority within constitutional terms and conditions established with the consent of the States; the participation of States' representatives in the exercise of the central political authority; and the participation of direct representatives of the people in the exercise of that authority. All these conditions are met now to some extent in the Community but it has become increasingly recognised that there must be institutional changes if only to take account of new developments. I have dealt with that problem at length in Chapter III. What can be excluded are ideas of pure

109

inter-governmentalism on the one hand and those of a unitary (or 'federal') super-state on the other. But the conditions I have stated are not incompatible with one another as is often supposed and, though they may be difficult to apply in practice, they are not impossible and do answer practical needs. One essential principle of this sort of federalism is that people should be represented both by directly elected representatives and by State governments.

One change that has been recommended is to provide for more effective executive authority at a Community level on the lines considered in Chapter III. There has been a marked tendency to conceive of such authority in terms of government of the unified, even personalised, form that has become so prevalent in the Member States themselves. It is true that executive authority probably needs to be lodged in a distinct institution and one distinct from both representatives of State governments and those elected directly by the people. This would exclude at least one of the Commission's future models for European Union, that with an executive consisting of ministers of State governments.[5] But what if we adopt as a ground rule a notion of government for the Community, not as something exclusive to an executive authority, but shared among a number of institutions?[6] This is not to suggest a literal revival of traditional notions of the separation of powers based on legislative, executive and judicial functions, which Chapter IV has shown to be wanting. Not just different functions but also processes, organisational principles, and interests must be recognised in forming the government of a complex system like the Community. In the Member States, as in other parts of the world, the development of modern, post-industrial government has made it far more difficult to realise such a separation of powers in practice. But need those problems arise, at least with the same historical force, in a Community government? It depends to some extent at least what we want it to be. The separation of powers among the four Community Institutions should not be abandoned, therefore, simply because the principle has been undermined elsewhere, since it could well provide a form of government especially suited both to the idea of parliamentary democracy and the Community's needs.

Another necessary change is to develop means by which the people acting as a body politic can, through free elections and representative institutions, determine the conditions according to which government is exercised. In this respect, there has been a tendency to reduce the political needs of the Community to those of improved communication between the Community and the public—both general as public opinion, and specialised as organised regional, social and economic interests. Thus the future role of the Parliament has been seen as important, less in terms of its status and powers, than in those of its 'educative, informative and communicative functions' and providing greater 'visibility and intelligibility in Community politics.[7] Such a view overlooks certain

---

[5] EC Commission, Bulletin of the European Communities, supplement 5/75, paras. 98–100.

[6] See, for example, A. Grosser, The Evolution of European Parliaments, *Daedalus*, 93, 1, 1965, p. 178.

[7] See, for example, V. Herman and J. Lodge *The European Parliament and the European Community*, (London, 1978), pp. 73–93.

vital requirements of legitimacy. The needs of a European polity include opportunities for influence and control by different interests and views affected by Community decisions, the means of reconciling such diverse elements into an acceptable view of the common interest, and the possibility of testing confidence in a responsible government. As my exploration of the circumstances following direct election has hinted, treating the Parliament simply as a venue for expressing differences could simply exacerbate fundamental divisions. At the least, it would fail to resolve the dissatisfaction of those who reject the Community because it gives them too little voice in deciding its form and content. The value of the Parliament as an instrument in forming a body politic depends, therefore, on its acquisition and use of powers.

From these ground rules, and from the political circumstances already outlined, the directly elected European Parliament would be well advised to look much more for its model to the US Congress—in particular the House of Representatives—than to the parliaments of the Member States. It is true that in terms of federalism and the role of representatives of the States' governments in central government, the Federal Republic of Germany offers relevant experience from within the European Community. It is likely that many features of the European Parliament's role—especially in relation to the Council—will continue to borrow from contemporary and past German federal experience. In non-Community Europe the Swiss popular chamber, the National Council, offers other interesting analogies: it operates at a level of government with constitutionally defined and limited powers, with a collegial executive serving a fixed term and it faces a multi-party system requiring inter-party compromise and power-sharing as an integral rule in both legislature and executive. The National Council is a bilingual (sometimes trilingual) assembly, in which a complex set of loyalties and interests—political, cultural, social, economic, linguistic, regional and cantonal—cut across parliamentary group lines. In content these divergences are far more analogous to those appearing in the European Parliament than would be those outside Western Europe. Nevertheless, in other respects the physiognomy of the Parliament is far closer to that of the US House of Representatives.

They are assemblies with a similar number of members, (435 in the House of Representatives since 1912, 410 in the European Parliament after 1978), a similar ratio of members to population, a comparable geographical distance of members from the electorate, and a comparable diversity of constituencies. The directly elected European Parliament will not (at least at first) have the two party system that has been so essential in explaining the physiology of US government but there are striking analogies in the decentralised nature of power within both assemblies and the lack of decisively polarised ideological differences. The political life of the European Parliament, like that of the Community as a whole, resembles in many respects the 'government of whirlpools' depicted by observers of Congress.[8] The earlier history of the House of Representatives (from inde-

---

[8] S. K. Bailey *Congress makes a law* (New York, 1950); E. S. Griffith *Congress: its contemporary role* (Washington DC, 1964), especially p. 55.

pendence to the civil war) may be even more analagous. The play of politics required a cast of figures from widely differing backgrounds and interests who performed on a stage of government of which by no means all the actors took the same view, even of whether the government should take the form it did.[9] There is a tendency for European observers to under estimate the importance even in Congress today of State, regional and local identities. Its special character as a parliamentary institution is still, above all, its inability to 'think nationally'.[10]

Analogies of this kind can be no more than illustrative. The powers and organisation of the popular chambers in both the USA and Switzerland—to take two relevant examples—like those of most parliaments in the Member States, are based on liberal ideas of government belonging to the late eighteenth or early nineteenth centuries. In both those countries, in spite of their contrasting physical, economic and political geography, the growth in importance of central government has tended to erode that basis. In both countries, in spite of great differences in the nature of politics in general and in that of the popular chambers in particular, the need for reform to reassert the power of the legislature and check that of the executive has been a continuing theme—in the last decade in Switzerland, and for much longer in the USA. There is no comparison, moreover, with the extremely limited constitutional basis of political authority that belongs to the European Community. Nor is there any comparison (at least under the present Swiss and US constitutions) with the role of States' representatives at Community level. The US Senate and the Swiss Council of States may have owed their origins to an intention that states' representatives should participate directly in government at a federal level but today they act mainly as second chambers of a directly elected legislature and are not therefore comparable to the Community's present Council.

The purpose of such analogies is not, therefore, to suggest that the ground rules have been so successfully developed elsewhere that there are ready made models to copy. It is to show that in trying to make a success of those rules in the circumstances open to us we are not confined to the models of a parliamentary assembly derived from experience in the Member States. None of what has been said, moreover, can dilute the basic assumption that the Community is *sui generis* and, moreover, in embryo. The choices remain open, and will partly depend on political contingencies.

There is some freedom, therefore, to choose whether the growth of central government, and of the executive branch in particular, that has occurred in most liberal democratic regimes with constitutional foundations of federal or unitary, presidential or parliamentary type, need recur at the Community level. There is also some freedom to choose whether a fresh attempt should be made to implement the ideas of parliamentary democracy—at least at a European level, or whether the alternative ideas of populism and corporatism taking hold in the

---

[9] A vivid and strikingly relevant account of the Jeffersonian era is given in James Young *The Washington Community 1800/1828* (New York and London, 1966). See also R. F. Nichols *The invention of the American political parties* (New York, 1967).

[10] G. B. Galloway *The legislative process in Congress* (New York, 1953) p. 668.

States will be allowed to spread to the Community. Thus the European Parliament needs to define its future role, not only using a wider palette than that provided by the existing Member States but also keeping a firm sense of perspective. In what follows I shall look in turn at some crucial aspects of the role of parliaments to indicate the sort of matters on which choices could be made.

Parliament's relations with the public

This aspect is important, both because there is a widespread impression that parliaments are held in low public esteem and because there are changing notions of what the relationship between parliament and people should be. What is at stake, however, is far more than shrewd use of information services to coax the mass media and to titillate public interest: it is the nature of representation itself. We know far too little about what the modern mass public demand and expect as individuals from government as a whole and parliament in particular at State level and we know even less in relation to the Community. The European Parliament should ask itself (and could consider commissioning research to help it) three particular questions: what are its members expected to represent; what kind of representation are they expected to provide; and how are they expected to account for what they do? That is not to suggest that public opinion should be decisive in answering those questions. It is to recommend that greater knowledge about public attitudes and expectations could dispel some illusions and clarify the task of defining the individual member's function towards his public.

I shall not go here into the several theoretical problems surrounding the idea of representation as it is applied in parliamentary assemblies but draw out three particular alternative views that are relevant to deciding what a directly elected member of the European Parliament might be considered to represent.[11]

He might be considered, first, to represent a political party and that will be the assumption with which most of the first members begin. I have dealt in Chapter IV with the way the prevalence of parties in the Member States has tended to produce a kind of direct democracy in which the MP acts rather as a party delegate in a plebiscitary system than as a genuine representative. Such a role of parties can be defended as clarifying issues for an electorate that would otherwise be unable to make choices among alternative policies and leaders. In both multi-party States in the Community and in the USA a polarised and disciplined party system on the supposed British model has been greatly envied by would-be reformers. Many might feel that the European Community should go the same way. At present, however, given the nature of the electoral procedure and the absence of real European political parties, it is difficult to see how party representation could be meaningful to the electorate unless it is on a State basis. We might well ask secondly, therefore, whether State representation will not become more important after direct election and the answer must clearly be in the affirmative for some members. But the representation of State parties (especially, but not only, when these are not in State government) will be extremely unsatisfactory,

---

[11] For a summary see A. H. Birch *Representation* (London, 1971), pp. 50–105.

since any one of them will always be heavily outnumbered in the European Parliament. Moreover, although members will to some extent inevitably act as State delegations, the importance of cross national issues and interests and the tradition of the Parliament itself, will work strongly against a lasting division of members on purely State lines. The place for representation of State interests is after all in the Council, and parliamentary representation will belie its purpose if the European Parliament becomes an assembly essentially of State delegations.

The most appropriate and, in time, probably the predominant type of representation, will be a third variety, that of districts, regions and localities. This is another respect in which the European Parliament will resemble the US House of Representatives.[12] Although the influence of districts on Representatives is often regretted in the literature on Congress, reformers in Europe have increasingly argued for closer ties between the member of parliament and his constituency. Whether such a diminution of party representation is likely or desirable must depend on how one views the role of existing political parties. They are important both for expressing a distinct State interest and for defending particular sets of political forces and ideologies or of special interests. It would be most unusual if some political groupings did not continue in some form in the European Parliament in the future. What precise form any future party system should take, however, and its influence on the relationship between members and their electorate, are matters for the time being where we can exercise some choice.[13]

There is a tendency to suppose that the new members of the European Parliament should adopt what might be called a senatorial as opposed to a tribune role, rather along the lines of what de Tocqueville saw as the distinction between the 'statesmanlike' Senators and 'vulgar' Representatives in the USA.[14] There has been considerable publicity and, in Community circles much welcome, for the news that certain notable individuals in national politics expect to stand for the first direct election. The presence of such figures promises to reinforce the Parliament's expected role as a 'grand forum' where the major issues of the Community and its future can at last be argued out in the public eye.[15] Such a role of public education is undoubtedly important and can act in a limited way as a counter to the secrecy of most crucial Community proceedings in the Council and

---

[12] See for example R. L. Peabody and N. W. Polsby *New Perspectives on the House of Representatives* (Chicago, 1973) Third Ed. pp. 3–26.

[13] In the USA much of the reform literature at least since the second world war (and even before) has argued for a strengthening of party identification and loyalty as opposed to fractionalism in Congress. There too the British model has been envied by some. See especially: American Political Science Association, *Towards a more responsible two-party system* (New York, 1950); R. H. Davidson & W. J. Oleszek *Congress against itself* (Bloomington, Indiana, 1977); L. N. Rieselbach *Congressional Reform in the Seventies* (Morristown NJ, 1977) pp. 67–110. On recent reforms to strengthen the role of the party caucus, see J. S. Clark *Congressional Reform* (New York, 1965); Rieselbach *op. cit.*, pp. 41–60.

[14] A. de Tocqueville *La Democratie en Amerique* Vol. II 14th ed. (Paris, 1864) pp. 52–3. See also the distinction between 'cosmopolitans' and 'locals' in H. D. Price's contribution to D. B. Truman (ed.) *The Congress and America's Future* (Englewood Cliffs NJ, 1965), pp. 50–1.

[15] For example in P. Allott The democratic basis of the European Community in *Common Market Law Review* Vol. II, August, 1974 pp. 321–5; Herman and Lodge *loc. cit.*

in meetings of heads of governments. But there is a tendency to beg the question whether the general public either expect this role to be performed by their representatives or will pay much attention to it. Although parliamentary reformers have argued at national level for more great debates on topical issues, it is doubtful whether the man in the street will ever share the fascination of the academic and the practised politician for the theatre of parliamentary debate, however it is conducted and portrayed. The reason why the proceedings of the European Parliament (as of most parliaments) are so boring in the media's sense of the word is partly that the subject matter of modern government is boring in that sense (it requires effort to understand it) and partly that the parliamentary aspect of public proceedings is often futile anyway in terms of bringing results. People themselves may be more shrewd than the informed elite give them credit for and may recognise that a working institution is better than an assembly of 'empty speeches'.[16]

At national level, students of parliament have come increasingly to believe that what people demand most from their parliamentary representatives is a kind of social service designed to respond to their individual complaints and anxieties about the public administration. In the European Parliament such a role will not be so important, since the bulk of public administration that affects people directly exists (and will continue) at State level. On the other hand, decisions of law and its implementation taken at a Community level in particular spheres are of vital direct importance for groups of citizens within the States, especially at regional and local level. In particular this applies to the operation of powers under the Coal and Steel Community Treaty, under the Common Agricultural Policy, the Regional and Social Funds, and under the Customs Union.[17] We can expect there to be great pressure on members of the Parliament to act as spokesmen for interests affected in this way. It is a vital role, given what I have said about the importance of the allocation of resources for the Community's future development. It means that public oratory will continue to be less important for the Parliament than application to the details of legislative and budgetary procedure. In other words, the kind of representative most people can be expected to want, and deserve, is a committee man rather than a debater, a fox rather than a lion.

That may present a problem for the Parliament's accountability to the public, for it may intensify the remoteness that geographical circumstances will already impose. We need then a practical view of the individual member's role that is different from what we have come to accept in most of the Member States. A far greater responsibility for maintaining relations with the public will have to rest personally on the European member than is normally exercised by most members of State parliaments now, especially in view of the geographical conditions. Three particular measures are suggested by that. First, the term of office fixed by the Decision of 1976 is too long at five years and should be shortened. That could be done at the same time as, secondly, the introduction of a uniform electoral

---

[16] From the telling irony of one of Joseph Conrad's characters in *Nostromo* (London, 1904), p. 202.
[17] See Fitzmaurice *op. cit.*, pp. 125–30.

procedure based entirely on regional and local constituencies. Thirdly, members should be allowed personal staffs paid out of Community funds, who could devote themselves, on the lines of the US Congress, largely to constituency work.[18]

Such measures are more important for creating public interest in the Parliament than expenditure on public relations in the modern sense. Publicity of proceedings too often means not greater public interest and participation but simply an enhancement of the role of the media, which in turn engenders among members a view of topicality and accountability that we have no reason to regard as necessary to parliamentary democracy (and some reason to regard as alien to it). But the Parliament should continue to practise the extremely liberal attitude to physical public access that it has done up to now, even if its members become more self important and its proceedings more significant. It will undoubtedly have to introduce stricter rules of lobbying (it seems to have hardly any now), if only for the sake of tolerable working conditions for members and staff and also for reasons I shall come to in the next section.[19]

The US House of Representatives has gone to considerable lengths in recent years to extend the public nature of its proceedings, so that ninety per cent of all committee meetings now take place in public and the public recording of voting has been extended. The effect of such measures can be to weaken party discipline which in the US system makes government all the more difficult.[20] That factor will be less relevant in Europe until we know more about what parties we want but taken to extreme lengths publicity can destroy the whole purpose of using committees. Public hearings, however, are being used increasingly by parliamentary committees to improve parliament's 'educational' function and could be extended to ensure much greater public comment (both favourable and unfavourable) on Community measures before these are enacted by the Council. Like other forms of mere publicising, however, it can actually lead to public disinterest if it is not related to actual decisions about public policy. In general, therefore, engaging public interest and serving it, probably requires above all a Parliament whose members can have an effective influence and control through formal powers.

Parliament and social and economic interests
The characteristic feature of pluralistic, constitutional regimes, according to Raymond Aron, is 'a dissociation of social and economic power from political power'.[21] If that is so, then the growing implication of government in economic affairs, and the related growth in political influence of organised social and

---

[18] See H. W. Fox Jr. and S. W. Hammond *Congressional Staffs* (New York and London, 1977), pp. 44–5 and passim. In 1976 there were altogether about 10,000 personal staff in Congress, performing as well as constituency functions, those on behalf of Congressmen in Congress itself in relation to lobbies and in relation to the executive. See also Truman *op. cit.*, pp. 48–49.

[19] See David Wood, Problems of creating a new parliament *The Times* 17 April 1978.

[20] Rieselbach *op. cit.*, pp. 47–51.

[21] R. Aron *Democratie et Totalitarisme* (Paris, 1965), p. 151.

economic interests, must represent a major challenge. In Chapter IV, I included that development under the name of corporatism as a growing alternative to parliamentary democracy in Western Europe. It is a challenge, however, that presents itself in the Community primarily at State level, because it is still State governments which hold the key (rusty as it is) to economic policy. However, the interdependence of State governments and organised interests in economic affairs clearly helps to explain why it has been so difficult to develop more effective economic policy making at a Community level. Indeed, while certain organised economic interests are said to have been extremely influential in the establishment of the Common Market, support from organised interests and policy initiative from a Community level have subsequently coincided only in relation to agriculture and some other specialised sectors. With certain important exceptions, European interest groups are no more effectively organised in general terms and on a continuing basis than European political parties.[22]

Nevertheless that fact alone, in its consequences for the Community's inability to rise above a purely sectoral approach to economic policy and thus to encompass a wider range of interests, is a reason why the European Parliament must take account of the role of organised social and economic interests in the Community and of its own relationship to them. Particular organisations can and do have direct impact at European level, whether through their own activities (for example, multi-national corporations) or in relation to specific Community decisions (for example on agriculture, company law and other social and economic legislation, customs matters, energy policy and so on). Partly it is a problem of possible inactivity by Community institutions (as might be the case with respect to multi-national corporations); partly there is the likelihood of pressure on the Commission or on individual State governments by sectoral interests or even by individual private bodies. The Parliament should recognise, therefore, both the need for European organisation of social and economic interests, and the need to ensure that the relationship between them and political authority at a Community level is conducted in a way that is compatible with parliamentary democracy.

There are already signs however that some organised interests see the future development of the Parliament's role as a threat to their own influence.[23] Where that influence is established now mainly at the level of government within the Member States, supranationalism and the growth of direct Community representation may be regarded as at best irrelevant and at worst disabling. Some organisations, especially trade unions, also cling to the national dimension because of ties with political parties, as is partly the case in Britain, France and Italy. The national and political connections of interests must help to explain why the body provided at Community level for their representation, the Economic and Social Committee, has not been more effective either in engaging more of

---

[22] Roy Pryce *The Politics of the European Community* (London, 1973), pp. 187–91; J. Meynaud and D. Sidjanski *Les groupes de pression dans la communauté européenne* (Brussels, 1971); G. Ionescu *Centripetal Politics* (London, 1976).

[23] Fitzmaurice, *op. cit.*, pp. 93–5.

their commitment or in making a greater impact. That body is also limited, however, by its restricted consultative status and powers and above all by the general preference of organised interests for direct, informal pressure at the points where decisions are made. One question, therefore, is whether the European Parliament will develop powers itself to attract the intervention of European level interests and another is whether it will develop political parties with a similar effect.

In the USA organised interests do traditionally regard Congress as well as the executive as an important object of pressure, given its share in legislative and budgetary power but given also the weakness of party discipline. The dependence of members of Congress on the support of private organisations for electoral purposes, partly from the lack of other means of mobilising constituency backing, is one factor making the relationship mutual.[24] That factor is likely to be present for members of the European Parliament to a greater extent than it is for members of State parliaments in Europe. Meanwhile, individual political groups in the Parliament are not likely to be particularly attractive as agents of organised interests at European level, given that most important social and economic interests cut across different groups and, in any case, no one group is likely to command a sufficient number of seats either to sway the majority on enough issues itself or in an effective coalition. In any event the Parliament might well not be able or willing to develop a party system polarised along lines of social and economic interests.

All this suggests that any role the Parliament might play in engaging organised social and economic interests in the Community will tend to follow the pattern of Congress: it will depend a great deal on the Parliament's ability to affect the outcome of decisions important to the interests concerned and the resulting relationship will tend not to follow strict party lines but be a factor itself in determining alignments and coalitions. Given the importance of engaging interest groups in the Community as a method of making social and economic policy, the Parliament should not eschew such a role but it will have to take care to ensure that it does not thereby become merely a channel for the more powerful organisations or a means whereby the demands of special groups are so loud as to drown the voice of the common interest.

The role of political organisation in the Parliament could be decisive in this as in other respects but the following suggestions can be offered:

(i) The Parliament should consider adopting a set of rules governing its own members' relations with private interests—both corporations in the legal sense and voluntary associations. It is particularly important to establish common rules, if unfairness is not to result from allowing different State practices. The 1946 Legislative Reorganisation Act in the USA might be of interest here, as well as further comparative study of the rules applying in the different Member States. Rules governing financial support in elections could be laid down as part of a proposal for a uniform electoral procedure and would raise the question of

---

[24] Griffith, *op. cit.*, pp. 140–52.

Community financing of political activities which needs to be considered in its own right. Other aspects would be the registration of lobbies and the declaration of interests by members.[25]

(ii) The importance of the representation of social and economic interests should be recognised without discouraging their distinction from political representation and to this end, the Economic and Social Committee should be actively promoted by the Parliament; it should be seen not as a rival but as a counterpart. The general problem of finding a satisfactory role for this sort of body is too wide for the present study[26] but the Parliament could consider the possibility of regularly involving it in its own work on legislative and budgetary matters, for example by organising joint meetings of specialised committees.[27]

(iii) The Parliament should also, however, develop its own relations with organised interests. An increasingly popular way of doing so is by public hearings held by specialised committees. Experience in the US Congress suggests that public hearings can be double edged, if seen as a means of controlling the activity of interest groups which can use them for special pleading. The investigatory powers of committees can certainly degenerate into a device for magnifying special grievances and for victimisation.[28] But if used circumspectly by the Parliament they could provide a platform for the expression of interests at a European level especially when the Parliament gives its opinion on legislative proposals and even enable the Parliament to draw on interests as a source of support.

(iv) The relationship of specialised committees to organised interests is a general problem and has led to demands for reform in the USA particularly. The vital question of co-ordination and control of committees and of the nature of the internal hierarchy will be considered later. The Parliament's budget committee clearly has a vital role to play in this respect. But the need for aggregating interests, for balancing one sector against another, and for setting a general framework extends to economic policy itself. Just as the Community as a whole needs reinforced means of making and applying common economic policy, so the Parliament could take its own initiative by developing its present Committee on Economic and Monetary Affairs. The Joint Economic Policy Committee of Congress could be seen as a model. Although that Committee is little more in practice than a kind of study group without direct effect on government policy, it has served to build up, with the help of qualified staff, a body of economic expertise in Congress capable of taking its own independent view of economic

---

[25] On the USA see especially Clark, *op. cit.*, pp. 174 ff.; R. Bolling *House out of order* (New York, 1965), pp. 262 ff.; Rieselbach, *op. cit.*, pp. 25–28; Davidson and Oleszek, *op. cit.*, passim.

[26] See however G. Ionescu's contribution to B. Burrows, G. Denton and G. Edwards *Federal solutions to European problems* (London, 1977), pp. 71–84. See also the Economic and Social Committee's Opinion on European Union, CES 363/75, Brussels, 1975.

[27] Rapporteurs of the Economic and Social Committee do now attend meetings of some of the Parliament's committees, and there are arrangements for exchanging information.

[28] Galloway, *op. cit.*, pp. 628–43; Davidson and Oleszek, *op. cit.*; Griffith, *op. cit.*, pp. 145–67. On Switzerland, see C. Hughes *The Parliament of Switzerland* (London, 1962), pp. 34–40; and E. Gruner (ed.) *Die Schweizerische Bundesversammlung 1920/68* (Bern, 1970).

policy.[29] Such a body in the Parliament could play an especially important role by public hearings of major 'peak' interests at both Community and State level.

However, no parliament seems to have overcome successfully the problem that economic policy in the modern, industrialised state is an executive prerogative.[30] In the Community there is the added complication that only halting steps have been made towards the effective co-ordination of national economic policy making, in spite of recent progress towards a common monetary system. But the Parliament's essential contribution both in engaging organised interests at European level and in controlling their activity may well lie chiefly in its ability to exercise legislative and budgetary power.

Parliament and legislation

Legislative powers are of fundamental importance for the European Parliament for three main reasons. In general the importance of the legislative functions of parliaments has been under estimated; the growth of discretionary executive power especially in economic affairs and the change in the nature of law making from a means of limiting, to a means of enabling, governmental activity should not weaken the general principle that legislation, and the participation of parliament in it, has a vital role in controlling the activities of public authorities.[31] Secondly, formal law plays a particularly important role in the Community and the rule of law is a vital ground rule of the treaty framework. Thirdly, Community legislation is for the most part a means for defining the relative competences of the Community and its Member States and will therefore continue to be essential in the Community's future development.

The Parliament, therefore, should regard a strengthening of its legislative powers as a primary objective. But in doing so it should avoid any aspirations of becoming a supreme legislative body; its powers are fundamentally restricted by the scope of the treaties and also by the rights in Community legislation of the other Institutions. Thus it would be wise to seek to extend its powers incrementally in two particular respects. First, it should lay particular stress on certain types of legislation. We have seen both that its powers have been extended in legislation having financial consequences and also that there is scope for a further extension in relation to legislation proposed under article 235 (as was proposed by the Vedel group) and article 155 (for delegating powers to the Commission).[32] The Vedel group also laid particular stress on the need to extend the Parliament's powers in legislation with constitutional effect, and the Parliament has in fact been recognised as having special rights with regard to legislation affecting direct elections, so this area might also be added.

Secondly, there is the question of what means it should use. Most previous

---

[29] See H. C. Mansfield's contribution to Truman, *op. cit.*

[30] A conclusion drawn from a forthcoming publication by PSI of a collaborative study undertaken by the Committee of Co-operation for European Parliamentary Studies on Parliaments and Economic Affairs.

[31] See, for example, T. Lowi *The End of Liberalism*, (New York, 1969), p. 144.

[32] See pp. 60–62.

proposals have envisaged amendment of the treaties but that is, of course, a cumbersome and risky method. It might be far more efficient and prudent to see how far the Parliament can go, in co-operation with the other Institutions, within the terms of the present treaties. The political weight of the directly elected Parliament itself will be a factor. The further development of its special constitutional relationship with the Commission and the possibilities of gaining support, in relation to particular substantive as much as general constitutional matters, among individual State governments could also be imporant.[33]

It is essential, above all, to be clear about what is intended by increasing the Parliament's legislative powers. It is not to empower the Parliament directly and formally to coerce the States' governments into accepting measures against their will.

There is no way short of unforeseeable political and constitutional change in the Community of avoiding the need to 'negotiate' measures with the representatives of State governments. The point of attack should be the governments' claim to an exclusive right to decide what is an adequate negotiation and on what terms measures should be blocked or allowed through. In particular, a minority national interest should not be allowed by means of veto and delay to defend a status quo tilted in its favour, without being made to take responsibility for its actions. We need, therefore, to consider the precise points of the legislative process at which the Parliament's intervention is both reasonable and necessary.

Initiative. The Tindemans report in the context of European Union proposed that 'the Council should immediately allow the Parliament to take initiatives by undertaking to consider the resolutions which the Parliament addresses to it'.[34] In fact there is a precedent for such a power in that it is the Parliament that proposes under article 138 measures for introducing a uniform electoral system. But the Parliament does anyway take initiatives in practice and could do so more, by passing resolutions even on matters for which it has not been asked for an Opinion, for example following the report of one of its committees. Such a committee report can be designed to propose a legislative measure. The question is whether it is necessary to empower the Parliament (by common agreement or by treaty amendment) to put resolutions directly to the Council for its consideration. What would this add to the character of Community legislation as a means of defining a coherent, rational and responsible view of the Community's future needs that is not already available, or could be available, from the Commission's

---

[33] Both the advantages and disadvantages of forming alliances with particular State governments are illustrated by the 1979 budgetary exercise which took place in 1978. In the Council the British and Italian governments supported the Parliament's amendments increasing the regional fund and thus enabled the Parliament eventually to uphold its amendments (on the basis of the rules of qualified majority voting and the rules governing the timing of decisions on the Budget). However, the British government has subsequently sought, along with other governments to over rule the Parliament's decision on the extraordinary grounds that, while it supports the Parliament's objectives on the regional fund, it does not want the Parliament to pursue them! If similar procedures were extended to Community legislation, therefore, the Parliament's ability to use alliances with governments would depend on the latter's general attitude to its own powers.

[34] EC Commission, Bulletin of the EC, Supplement 1/76 p. 29.

right of proposal? Parliament's ability to indicate the need for legislation on particular matters of interest to special groups could be met in addition to own initiative committee reports through such means as petitions and questions, backed by its power to hold the Commission accountable. However, if it did develop a significant power of legislative initiative, it would make itself unique among parliamentary assemblies. Even in the US Congress the initiative has for some time now effectively passed to the executive.[35] Concentration on this power could well distract from more important needs.

Amendment. Even the potential of the Parliament's existing right to give an Opinion on Commission proposals should not be under estimated, especially if it were used more fully to give an opportunity to different interests to publicise their views by means, for example, of public hearings by the Parliament's committees. Given the now general agreement that the Parliament's power to propose amendments should be extended to all legislative proposals made by the Commission under the treaties, the next step could be for the Commission to agree to accept all the Parliament's amendments passed by an agreed majority and put revised proposals to the Council. That would certainly require from the Commission a more active political role in relation to the Parliament but that in itself need be no bad thing, if it is seen as part of a general strategy by the Commission to base its proposals on a body of political support in the Parliament. The problem is, as we have seen, what happens to the amendments when they are proposed to the Council.

Second Reading (suspensive veto). Once it is ensured that the Parliament's amendments are considered by the Council, the next step is to ensure that the Parliament has an opportunity to reconsider the proposal concerned after the Council has pronounced on the amended version. There are vital reasons for such a procedure, which was also recommended by the Vedel group. One is that the Council could be obliged by the Parliament to explain why it has taken up the position it has. At present it answers collectively to no one and it is hardly even obliged to make a decision on Parliament's amendments at all, except in financial legislation. It may and does also amend proposals itself in other ways that the Parliament would not accept. A second reading would seem to be essential, therefore, if the Parliament is to have any opportunity at all to intervene effectively in the legislative process. It would also serve, if properly used, to force much greater openness on Council proceedings, if only as a result of inquiries after the event and it would make the position of blocking minorities far more uncomfortable politically.

Conciliation. This procedure, as we have seen, has already been developed for legislation with long term financial implications and it should be extended, following second reading, to the sort of legislative categories mentioned earlier. It has the advantage of enabling the Parliament to form alliances with particular

---

[35] 'Since 1933 . . . the initiative in formulating legislation, in asserting legislative priorities, in arousing support for legislation, and in determining the final content of legislation enacted has clearly shifted to the executive branch'. S. P. Huntington in Truman, *op. cit.*, p. 23.

governments' representatives or groups of them and of seeking, which is the main object, a compromise designed to serve the general interest. Such a procedure is normal, for example, in the relations between first and second chambers in the Federal Republic of Germany, Switzerland and the USA. It has the disadvantages, however, that the participants in the conciliation procedure may be unrepresentative, may carry insufficient authority and may tend to rewrite legislation in a lengthy and enclosed procedure that produces a compromise welcomed by no one and accepted only by default.[36] In the Community there is the problem that the legislative process is already notoriously prone to deliver package deals based on the lowest common denominator, often thrown together in desperation and with any clear cut issues having been lost early in the process, if they get resolved at all.

Veto (co-decision). It is further essential, therefore, to require conciliation committees to report back on their work, and for the Institutions concerned to pronounce upon it. That is why ultimately the Parliament must be provided, as the Vedel group proposed, with a power of 'co-decision', in effect a power of veto.[37] By the same means, the timing of legislative procedure can be controlled and it should be for the Commission in making proposals to include provisions (amendable by both Parliament and Council) laying down a timetable for their consideration in the various stages. If either Parliament or Council ultimately veto a proposal, then the procedure needs to begin again. Of course this seems a dangerously negative way of approaching the Parliament's legislative powers, especially given that many of its members will want to pass, not reject, measures, and that it is the governments who usually apply the veto. That brings us back immediately to the issues discussed in Chapter III. The fact is that we have to get right away from the idea of coercing governments by legal means into taking political decisions which is totally unrealistic. In the end, acceptable Community legislation has to be the product of political compromise including the governments. But there can be compromise to do nothing, compromise to protect special interests, and compromise to further the general interest by action. Parliament's veto power should therefore be seen in a positive sense as a means of raising the level of negotiation and imposing accountability for inaction. The Commission and the governments should have to consider from the beginning of the legislative process and be constantly reminded during it, that Parliament's views have to be incorporated. In practice, the effect should make it unnecessary even to reach the final stages of legislative procedure as defined here, perhaps even unnecessary to go to a second reading. Much depends of course on the nature of the Parliament's relationship with the Commission and on its own internal organisation, including the question of what sort of majorities should be regarded as carrying effective authority to justify accepting parliamentary amendments.

---

[36] EC Commission, Bulletin of the EC, Supplement 4/1972 Ch. IV sec, IV para. 4.
[37] C. Sasse, *Decision making in the European Community*, (New York and London, 1977), pp. 346–48.

Parliament and the executive

Legislative power may be necessary but it is by no means sufficient for ensuring responsible government, especially in modern circumstances where the discretionary powers of the executive can be so vital for essential aspects of public policy. Four aspects of what might be called executive authority need particular consideration if the Parliament is to seek realistically to participate in Community government: the budget; economic policy; foreign policy; and the Parliament's general relations with the Commission.

The Budget

The Parliament's role in relation to the Community budget has become, as we have seen, its most important means of intervention. Its role is simplified compared with that of most State parliaments by the fact that the Community budget is not, as yet at least, an economic instrument in the way State budgets need to be regarded nowadays. However, to quote the Commission's report on European Union, the budget could come 'to play an important role in transferring resources between the (national) economies and in redistributing them between social groups so as to eliminate imbalances'.[38] In the short term it could be given greater importance for economic policy as was discussed in Chapter III, as a structural instrument and as an integral part of the European Monetary System.

Thus the Parliament's veto power over the budget could be used in an effort to influence and control the overall choices about economic intervention by the Community, in spite of the existing limitations on its power of amendment. As a result, however, the Parliament would be exercising a role in budgetary matters far more extensive than that normal in State parliaments and as a condition it would have to eschew the incrementalism typical of most budgetary procedures.[39] We have seen that the Parliament is already trying to use its budgetary powers as a policy instrument. If it intends to go further in that direction, to seek to enforce its own spending priorities and to treat the annual budget in terms of the basic choices it implies, it will be performing a service for the Community that the other Institutions have not so far proved capable of doing. But it will need to accept both a growing predominance within its own committee hierarchy for the budget committee and a substantial increase in staffing. The example of Congress could yet again be instructive here, since in recent years, especially with the development of the Congressional Budget Office, Congress has come, in the view of at least one observer, to match the expertise of the executive branch and to become something like an equal partner with it in budgetary matters.[40]

However, there remain other more fundamental limitations to be overcome and the Parliament should not try to overreach itself. Its budgetary powers, highly significant as they are, cannot do the job on their own. First, as we have seen, legislation is required to make more flexible the sources of Community

---

[38] EC Commission, Bulletin of the EC, Supplement 7/57 paras. 43–6.
[39] The issues are discussed in a useful summary in Ann Robinson *Parliament and public spending*, (London, 1978), pp. 1–24.
[40] Rieselbach, *op. cit.*, pp. 51–6.

revenue and borrowing (where ratification by the States may be necessary), as well as the introduction of the means of Community intervention that do not consist purely of the reimbursement of State expenditure but represent some conscious set of Community social and economic objectives. Even so, the Parliament can still be frustrated by the absence of legislative authority to allow expenditure to be made once approved. That is not only a technicality; it rests on the fact that the overall composition of the budget arises from serious political choices that are not easily made or unmade in the context of expenditure decisions themselves. The problem of agricultural expenditure highlights that. Indeed, the Parliament itself is likely to find it very difficult in practice to take more than an essentially incremental approach, even though its members have a common interest in trying to treat the budget as a whole.[41] Given that the Council will continue to insist on cutting the initial budget proposal incrementally and that many members of the Parliament will be interested for constituency purposes in making increases in specific types of expenditure, it will be extremely difficult for the Parliament itself (through its budget committee in the first instance) to take a programmatic view, let alone to make it prevail.

In this respect, the role of an executive authority is crucial and in this case it can only be the Commission. Acting in response to expected parliamentary budgetary demands and in the light of parliamentary opinions regarding the desirable purposes and methods of expenditure in terms of need and efficiency (expressed through its subject committees), the Commission should present a form of budget that is more than a mere accounting record of haphazard decisions made by the Council. Such a proposal would need to be based, however, on a conscious set of policy choices that would itself need to be debated and approved separately if the budgetary proposal were to be at all realistic.[42]

Economic policy

Apart from the highly embryonic public expenditure powers represented by the budget, the Community is notoriously lacking in specific instruments for economic intervention. The treaties deal with economic policy only indirectly and it is an area where the Community relies overwhelmingly, even since the halting decisions towards economic and monetary union, on co-ordination and co-operation among the States' governments themselves. The original Werner proposals envisaged a decision centre for economic policy politically responsible before the Parliament in the final stage of economic and monetary union but it was far from clear what the powers of such a body would be or what form its responsibility would take. The fact remains, however, that even short of the final measures envisaged by Werner (like a common currency, common central

---

[41] On the problems see especially A. Wildawsky *Budgeting: a comparative theory of budgetary processes*, (Boston, 1975), pp. 23–46, and pp. 201–50.
[42] This is illustrated by Parliament's attempts to increase incrementally the regional and other funds for structural intervention in recent years, and particularly in the constitutional crisis provoked by its action on the 1979 Budget, see note 32 above. On the importance of the Community Budget for planning, however, see Sasse, *op. cit.*, pp. 229–33.

banking arrangements and so on) a common monetary policy will ultimately rest on decisions of economic policy. What steps are to be taken when things go wrong and States are faced either with leaving the currency system or imposing politically unacceptable measures internally?[43]

Even if instruments of economic policy making were developed at a Community level, however, we would have to recognise that everywhere—even in the USA where Congress seems to be more advanced in this respect than European national parliaments—the way those instruments are used and co-ordinated rests with the executive.[44] Control of the money supply, exchange rate policy, tariffs, and above all prices and incomes policy normally evade effective parliamentary control.[45] There are ways, however, in which Parliament could by concerted action influence and control economic policy through its budgetary and legislative powers: fiscal measures, Community expenditure to allocate resources, control of Community borrowing powers and so on. It will need to be vigilant to those ends and should study the possibilities of developing parliamentary control even of other instruments. As a preliminary suggestion an extension of conciliation procedure could allow meetings between Parliament's economic and monetary committee and the Council, when the latter is dealing with general economic and monetary questions. For the time being, however, like its State counterparts, the Parliament seems to be limited to using its formal powers to ensure that the Community has an executive that the Parliament can trust and ultimately hold accountable. It follows that decisions about the use of the relevant instruments (for example, borrowing and investment and other budgetary measures) should be vested in the same body, answerable to the Parliament and not in a variety of Community agencies and organisations (such as the European Investment Bank or in inter-governmental committees).[46] The need to recognise the Commission as the Community's executive is thus further reinforced.

Foreign policy

A similar conclusion seems appropriate where Parliament's role in foreign policy is concerned. The Community sphere has come to include that aspect of policy both through the Community's responsibility for external trade relations (on the basis mainly of the common customs tariff) and through the now regular meetings of foreign ministers and their officials in european political co-operation. The Parliament has already established its own right to question and debate foreign policy as a Community matter (see Chapter II). It has demanded further powers, on the one hand, to ratify trade and association agreements before they are completed and even approve the mandate on which they are negotiated by

---

[43] See L. Tsoukalis, *The Politics of Economic and Monetary Integration* (London, 1977), pp. 31–48.
[44] Mansfield in Truman *op. cit.*
[45] See note 30, p. 120.
[46] On the Parliament's recent attempts to ensure accountable management of the Community's loan facilities, see European Parliament Debates, Official Journal No. 203 8 May 1978 p. 9. See also European Parliament Working Documents 1978/79, document 150/78.

126

the Commission. On the other hand, it wants to have more frequent colloquiums between its political committee and the foreign ministers and base these and plenary debate on a written rather than simply an oral report from the President of the Council.[47] Ultimately, however, a Parliament will find, as has the US Congress, that its political clout in foreign policy as in other matters will depend on its ability to use legislative and budgetary power to constrain indirectly the executive's role.[48] For the Parliament, therefore, an important issue must be what constitutes the executive at Community level for foreign policy. A clear recognition that, as in other matters, it is the Commission rather than the mooted political secretariat based in Paris, would obviously work in the Parliament's favour, given that the Commission is at least formally answerable to the Parliament through the latter's ultimate sanction of censure.

Relations with the Commission
Are we forced then to the general conclusion that the establishment of a proper Community executive must come before that of effective parliamentary powers? At least we can say that the Parliament will certainly have to ask itself where executive authority should and does lie, in order to make practical and meaningful decisions about its own role. I have already argued, first, that some central executive authority will have to be recognised and, secondly, that it cannot be formed from the States' governments themselves. It is unlikely, however, that the Parliament could create that executive out of itself, as some national parliaments have done (above all the British model), given the need to include the States' governments in the selection and the accountability of executive authority at Community level. It is also undesirable, if we are to have the sort of separation of powers that has been described as an essential ground rule of Community government. Indeed, parliamentary executives tend to undermine the independence and vitality of the parliaments from which they emerge. However, we should not harbour the illusion that a formal separation of executive and legislative authority, which has been established in different ways in the USA and Switzerland, overcomes the limitations on parliamentary influence and control imposed by modern circumstances of government. Congress has been by no means free from executive encroachment and superiority but there is a substantial literature bemoaning the effects of lack of party discipline, decentralised power within Congress and dislocation between legislative and executive leadership on the coherence and continuity of government in the USA.[49] The ingenious Swiss system of putting the executive virtually into commission, rather than

---

[47] European Parliament, Working Documents 1977/78, document 427/77, 13 December 1977.

[48] Rieselbach, *op. cit.*, pp. 21–23; N. J. Ornstein and D.W. Rodhe in Peabody and Polsby, *op. cit.*, pp. 252–61.

[49] Truman, *op. cit.*; Clark, *op. cit.*; Bolling, *op. cit.*; Griffith, *op. cit.*; Davidson and Oleszek, *op. cit.* In the last fifty years Congress has been in a variety of relationships to the executive: sometimes acting with greater independence of the Presidency (a role adopted particulary since the Watergate affair), sometimes with less (as under Lyndon Johnson). For alternative views of the role of Congress, see C. Rossiter, *Parties and Politics in America*, (Ithaca NY, 1960); R. Neustadt *Presidential Power*, (New York, 1962); and A. M. Schlesinger *Congress and the Presidency*, (New York, 1969); A. de Grazia (ed.) *Congress: the first branch of government* (Washington DC, 1966).

.ving it the special legitimacy afforded by direct, popular election, has not prevented concern about the decline of parliament's role in legislation and in control of the executive, given particularly the Federal Council's direct relationship with organised interests and with cantonal governments (as well as the use of the referendum).[50] Neither of these models offers reliable evidence that the idea of parliamentary democracy, implied by much of the European Parliament's own self unfolding, is made practical simply by providing a separation of powers.

What then are the possibilities of creating something original in the Community, which is, as we have seen, a polity, if at all, only in embryo? Certain needs are unavoidable. For effective budgetary planning, economic policy making and conducting relations with the rest of the world, not to speak of the task of ensuring that existing legislation is implemented and policy applied, there is need for an independent Community-level executive authority. Such a body needs, however, the political authority to be able to formulate realistic objectives and interpret the needs of an evolving social and economic union. It also has to fill the vital role of mediator, not only among State governments but also between them and the Parliament, as well as among organised interests and among political forces represented in the Parliament. The need for responsible government suggests that these functions should be vested in a single institution answerable to the Parliament. The ideal way forward, therefore, is to build on the role of the existing Commission, whose members need not be of or from the Parliament in order to be obliged to look to it for political direction and support, for supervision and criticism. As both the Vedel and Tindemans reports have proposed, the relationship between Commission and Parliament could be rationalised by giving the latter the right to confirm the appointment by the State governments of the President of the Commission as well as the power of dismissal it now has.[51] A further step would be to require the President also to get Parliament's confirmation of his selection of the other members of the Commission and of their collective programme of legislation and policy. How the relationship evolves in practice, however, and the relative weight of the two bodies, compared also with that of the Council, will depend on the sort of political organisation that is developed within the Parliament itself.[52]

---

[50] Secretariat de l'Assemblee Federale, Rapport intermediaire presenté aux Chambres Federales par la commission d'étude 'Avenir du Parlement', Bern, 17 March 1976.

[51] EC Commission, Bulletin of the EC, Supplement 1/76 pp. 29–30; Supplement 4/1972 Ch. IV sec. VII.

[52] This account has not dealt with the possible role of the Parliament in relation to what might be called the Commission's powers of delegated legislation—its right to enact measures acting alone (under article 155 for example) or subject to the control of management committees. Review of such executive activity might well become an additional function of the Parliament's committees (which may need sub-committees for the purpose). The only control at present is provided by management committees appointed by State governments, and ultimately judicial review. There is, however, a case for giving the Parliament some right of prior control of delegated legislation say, by empowering the Parliament which would act through its own committees—to give an opinion on certain types of measure, if it requested the right to do so within a certain delay and by a certain majority (and committees could if necessary report that a plenary debate and vote were necessary). See also European Parliament, Working Documents, loc. cit.

Parliament's internal organisation and power structure

A vital factor in the Parliament's future role, therefore, will be the way its members develop internally its character as an institution. One thing that is sure but often overlooked in discussions of the Parliament's future role, is that individual members will enjoy much greater scope in that respect than do those of parliaments within the nation states of Western Europe at the present time. As was explained in Chapter II the Parliament will exercise greater independence than State parliaments normally have in determining its own procedure and organisation. It might well set out, in fact, in the first year or two after the first election to test its power over such practical, but important matters as the payment of its members, their services and facilities and the establishment of a fixed seat for itself (in fact even though not in law).

In a wider sense its independence as an institution will be expressed when it establishes its own internal system of leadership and structure of power. For these matters will not be settled for the Parliament either by the election or by an executive with majority support among its members. To the extent that the executive is the Commission it rests with a separate collegial institution. The role of the Parliament's leadership, however, will be limited above all because the Parliament has to share its power, such as it is, with the other Community Institutions, particularly the Council, playing a far more predominant role in the Community's government than is typical of a federal second chamber representing State governments or legislatures. Moreover, whilst most of its members will probably devote a greater proportion of their time to the European mandate relative to others (and many will possibly devote all their time), there will be a variety of cross cutting loyalties and interests, relatively weak or absent party discipline, and strong ties with outside interests. In view of the possibilities outlined in this chapter, we can expect the Parliament to divide its time between concentrated work (conducted predominantly in specialised committees) on detailed and complicated business of finance and legislation on the one hand, and the airing of general economic and foreign policy issues through debates and questions on the other. The image of a working Parliament, rather than a mere debating assembly or 'talking shop' is likely to prevail, however, with a high degree of specialisation and even professionalism among members.

Staff—both institutional and personal—are likely to play an important role, both in relations between members and their electorate and in the day-to-day activities of the institution. And we must not forget that it will be a multi-lingual as well as multi-national assembly, so that interpretation and translation facilities will continue to be crucial.[53] There will be relatively little need for continuous control of public administration (which will still be conducted primarily within the States). However, it will be essential to maintain working relations with other institutions above all the Commission and Council and it is likely that geographical dispersion will present a problem.

All these factors suggest that the Parliament would be best to meet in intervals

---

[53] The Swiss Federal Assembly has found on occasions that unfortunate misunderstandings can arise when members of a multi-lingual assembly do not use such facilities.

of compressed sittings, on the model of the Swiss Federal Assembly, for about three weeks three or four times a year.[54] In any event its members are likely to come together for plenaries only for separate and limited periods (quite apart from vacations and recesses) and their own time will be divided among different activities, organs and venues. For all these reasons effective leadership of the Parliament could be vital. The effects of direct elections as envisaged and the absence of a system of European political parties will not make it any easier to obtain. Procedural matters could well be more contested than they have been up to now. The need to rely on specialised committee work could add greatly to the problems of co-ordination and internal management. The experience of the US Congress has illustrated some of the problems to watch out for: overlapping jurisdiction, multiplication of committees and sub-committees, growth of individual committee 'empires', a tendency of special interests to 'colonise' particular committees, and imbalances in workload.[55] Moreover, as we have seen, in order to make effective use of its powers, the Parliament will not only need a coherent and continuing strategy but also to be able to express itself by clear and substantial majorities. The existing formal provisions of a two-thirds majority for the vote of censure, and three-fifths for upholding amendments to the budget, plus in both cases an absolute majority of members, are particularly demanding. Discipline will be required, therefore, and a good record of attendance if powers are to be used or threatened meaningfully. Internal cohesion and co-operation will be a condition of many of the possible developments already considered.

In Chapter II we saw that up to now the Parliament's power structure has been based on its Presidency, supported by a consensus among 'elder statesmen' of the Parliament and the leaders of political groups. The personnel of this 'establishment' might or might not survive direct elections, and in any event the consensus might well be far more difficult to maintain in the institution as a whole. However, broadly the same type of power structure can be expected to continue, though it may be much looser and more complex and inconsistent: it might resemble the US Congress which has been described as 'a series of interlocking systems with power fairly well distributed'.[56] Given the collegial nature of the Commission as a separated executive and the inevitable multiplicity of political groups, however, the structure is likely to resemble even more in practice that of the Swiss National Council.[57] The need to achieve a consensus among several political groups, in addition to the other disparate elements described earlier, suggests that the authority of the enlarged bureau (as a sort of multi-party rules committee) is likely to be predominant. The President of the Parliament is

---

[54] However, that Assembly has found that members complain of insufficient time to prepare for business when sittings are extended over three weeks. At first, the European Parliament might not want to meet more than it does now—about one weekly sitting a month (sometimes two) for nine months of the year.

[55] See Davidson and Oleszek, *op. cit.*, pp. 6–10; Galloway, *op. cit.*, pp. 649–50; Bolling, *op. cit.*, pp. 59 ff.; Peabody and Polsby, *op. cit.*, pp. 139–67; 273–95.

[56] Griffith, *op. cit.*, pp. 25–6.

[57] See Gruner, *op. cit.*

unlikely to develop the personal authority of a Speaker Clay, nor is there likely to be a clear majority leadership.

Such a pattern might not be at all bad from the point of view of parliamentary democracy, especially in the refinement of the idea presented in Chapter IV of this study. It might be considered unsatisfactory, however, by those who stress what I have called a utilitarian view of the Community's development, and who see the Parliament's role either as reinforcing the executive leadership of the Commission, or throwing up its own political leadership, in order to lead the Community into further integration. What they would probably prefer to see is the emergence of a majority in the Parliament trying to perform the role attributed to the Federalists and later the Jeffersonians in the USA, or perhaps the Radical Party in Switzerland in the latter half of the nineteenth century: 'binding sections of the nation into an association capable of governing'.[58] However, in the circumstances of the Community, there must be considerable doubt whether—even with the external leadership of the Commission—such a majority could be formed effectively from the disparate elements that will make up the Parliament especially after direct elections. (Historians have mixed feelings about the result of similar efforts in the USA before 1828.)

From the point of view of democracy, as has been stressed repeatedly in this study, it is far from clear where the interests of the utilitarians really lie. Would a pro-integration majority leadership of the European Parliament seek to increase the latter's power to intervene in the government of the Community, if it threatened as it would to make the task of gaining agreement on new measures all the more complicated? As noted in Chapter II, there has already emerged a distinction between 'maximalists' and 'minimalists' in the Parliament on the question of powers and how they are used and concerted action is further obstructed by conflicting interests on substantive matters like agriculture.

In many ways a concerted strategy to increase the Parliament's power (in the sense of better use of existing powers and demands for more) would be more likely to come from an opposition than was concerned less with integration than with altering the Community's general economic consequences and the specific distribution of its expenditure. Direct election is likely to strengthen such opposition, though that may be too strong a description for what will undoubtedly be a random collection of individuals: some idealists but predominantly protectors of particular, sectional interests of economic group, region, nation and State. It would include, moreover, members (such as those of the British Labour Party) overtly opposed to any increase in the Parliament's power. The paradox of such opposition, however, is that in order to assert itself it would have to adopt a common strategy designed to tie substantive demands with procedural issues. In other words, it could use its position in the Parliament effectively only if it had some influence in the Parliament itself, especially if a conservative, gradualist majority emerges in coalescing to control key positions in the Parliament's

---

[58] Young, *op. cit.*, p. 124. See also Ralph V. Harlow, *The History of Legislative Methods before 1825* (New Haven, 1917); G. B. Galloway *History of the House of Representatives* (New York, 1961); R. Bolling *Power in the House* (New York, 1974); Peabody & Polsby, pp. 389–409.

internal leadership—committee chairmanships, Vice-Presidencies and the Presidency itself.

The efforts of such an opposition group could create an important new power structure cutting across and even destroying the political groups. Eventually such a 'democratic' party could well take general issue with the existing majority on the pace of constitutional change in the interests of parliamentary influence, and might find its ultimate path to power as lying through the introduction of a uniform electoral procedure. Thus, if a majority form of leadership dedicated to asserting the Parliament's role emerges at all, it might have some strange and unexpected roots.

Parliament's relations with other parliaments

In other words, many if not most directly elected members will find a very different political and institutional environment from parliamentary life in their own Member State. Adjustment will also be necessary to another aspect that will be strange to many, arising from the federal nature of Community government.The relationship among representative institutions at different levels of government is a general problem of increasing importance in Western Europe, in view not only of the development of the Community but also of that of regional and other levels of direct representation within States. It seems to be a feature of federal and regional systems of government that to co-ordinate their activities to the extent necessary in modern government, different levels resort to administrative means of decision making that exclude, or at least impede, parliamentary influence and control. How to overcome those limitations on the role of parliaments where government is divided among different levels is a subject where more knowlege is badly needed; it could be obtained by studying the experience of past and present federal and regional systems in Europe and elsewhere.[59]

Another reason why the European Parliament should think seriously about its relationship with State parliaments is that the latter's support will be necessary, not only directly for constitutional amendments to the treaties increasing the Parliament's powers but also indirectly for particular measures of law and policy. They are involved in the latter respect, because the State governments represented in the Community's Council normally need at least implicit parliamentary support at national level for the positions they take up in negotiations. Indeed, the role of national parliaments in Community law and policy making, while it is obviously confined by the provisions of the treaties and the supranational character of the Community, has been shown to be more important than many early accounts supposed.[60] Some national parliaments have developed special procedures for holding ministers accountable, while others use existing procedures. A major limitation, of course, is that national parliaments have ultimately to delegate power to ministers to act on their behalf and I have repeatedly referred in this study to the adverse consequences of that for democracy.

[59] But see the forthcoming preliminary study of this question by the Committee of Co-operation for European Parliamentary Studies to be published by PSI.

[60] See especially John Fitzmaurice *The party groups in the European Parliament* (London, 1975).

The relationship between ministers and State parliaments in Community matters depends also, however, on domestic politics. The members of the European Parliament would be wise to recognise that valuable influence can be exercised through parliaments within the States on Community decisions, especially if those parliaments can be persuaded to take an interest and to be active in Community business. Inversely, the more the European Parliament gets in on the act of legislation at Community level the better able it will be to provide information and opportunities for pressure which could be used by parliaments in the Member States. Public hearings by the Parliament's committees could be especially valuable in this respect.[61]

On the other hand, it is not necessary for State parliaments and the European Parliament to take the same majority view on particular issues or even on their general attitude towards the Community. Differences between them should be resolved where necessary through the relationship of Parliament and Council. There is not likely to be permanent or inevitable conflict between the European Parliament on the one hand and the Council representing national parliaments and governments on the other, or, for that matter between the Parliament and any particular State parliament. The various Institutions are not, and are not likely to become, so monolithic or inflexible. A varying and shifting pattern of coalitions can be expected involving political parties and other groupings in both the European Parliament and State parliaments. That is why the Parliament's members themselves will undoubtedly want means of keeping in touch with the attitudes of members of State parliaments on Community matters. Political parties will serve this purpose to some extent but in view of direct elections and the end of the double mandate for most members, there is probably a case for creating a special liaison office for relations with State parliaments in the Parliament's secretariat.

Indeed, although the sort of role for the Parliament envisaged here would certainly be expected to shift some of the focus of Community politics in its direction, the Council and inter-governmental relationships outside it would continue to be the main centre of Community decision making for as long as it is worth trying to see ahead. Most of the Parliament's own activity, therefore, must continue to be dominated by the problem of obtaining support from the Member States' governments. Successful measures will often be those that can be supported by a coalition of certain governments and substantial numbers of the Parliament's members. The relationship between Parliament and Council will certainly change, therefore, but will evolve in its own way depending on the sort of political alliances that are available and that can be put to work. At the same time members of the European Parliament will also need direct contacts with other levels of government within the Member States, increasingly important as these are becoming in certain States (in particular, Britain, Belgium and Italy). In fact, a double mandate might well develop between regional parliaments and the European Parliament and might become a means of providing the necessary

---

[61] The Swiss example, where relations between cantonal and federal parliaments have been eased by the wide practice of a double mandate, may be worth further study.

contact between them. But the Parliament could in general have a vital role in representing regional interests based on representative institutions in federal, regional or devolved State regimes. The question of Europe can also be seen, therefore, as one of finding the right level of government for different functions and also, no less importantly, one of limiting government at each particular level to make it more manageable. Working relations between parliamentary bodies at the different levels have a role to play in that, even though their functions will be different.

Conclusions
The future possibilities of the European Parliament have been discussed here from the perspective of a particular view of what parliamentary democracy requires in terms of institutional provisions. Such an exercise has called for a suspension of disbelief in certain respects. For example, some would maintain that the real problem facing the European Community is not the absence of parliamentary democracy but the limitations of the machinery for bringing about agreement among the State governments. Indeed, it could be argued that, by increasing the influence of centrifugal forces, a stronger Parliament could actually make the Community's problems worse. However, while the view of parliamentary democracy taken here may well not be shared by everyone, one conclusion is that the Community can develop more effective means of achieving consensus and realising common goals only if it deals in some way with the centrifugal forces that exist. For that reason a stronger Parliament, it has been argued here, is necessary for a more effective Community, though it is by no means sufficient, and will bring problems of its own.

Nevertheless, it can still be argued that something other than parliamentary democracy as understood here should be developed. The wider question of the viability of parliamentary democracy in circumstances of modern government goes beyond this study. But the question is a highly pertinent one, all the same, and it may be that most people, including the new members of the European Parliament, would prefer some other approach, whether out of political conviction or from a different diagnosis of the problem, or both. What has been attempted here is to show what the requirements of parliamentary democracy are, how they might be realised, and how they can be adapted to meet other requirements.

What the study has sought to stress, in fact, is that the future role of the European Parliament, like that of other parliamentary institutions, must depend to a large extent on the aims and attitudes of its own members, and in particular on the way political parties develop, if at all. If existing attitudes and patterns of behaviour in national politics prevail, then the European Parliament can be expected to go the same way as existing parliaments, which is generally—though by no means exclusively—into decline. On the other hand, if the opportunity for a new start is seized, and a directly elected European Parliament provides a much more promising opportunity than exists—or has existed for some time—in any of the Member States themselves, then we could witness an important revival of parliamentary democracy, one moreover that could recoil in its effects on the role of parliaments within the Member States. But a change of attitudes will be necessary, and a re-examination of first principles along the lines of what has been attempted here.

There is a double impediment to that since, not only is parliamentary democracy itself short of supporters (in other than name), but there are powerful forces now represented by some of the State governments which cannot countenance the development of democratic institutions outside the boundaries of the existing nation States. The fact that a form of government has already emerged outside those boundaries does not seem to have affected the obstinacy of those who believe that existing national sovereignties must be indivisible, and, in spite of all the evidence to the contrary, essential to democracy. There is no evidence that the people at large, when consulted, share that attitude, but powerful individuals and organisations within the political establishments of the States, for formidable grounds of self-interest, would not see that there was anything to be gained from the development of democracy in the Community. For that reason, the introduction of direct elections is but the beginning of the real struggle.

The study has also stressed, therefore, that the future of the European Parliament will depend to a large extent on its relationship with other institutions in both Community and States. Whatever the attitudes of the electorate and of the Parliament's own members, a change of approach will also be required by other, more powerful and enduring political forces. That calls for an elaborate form of concerted action among State governments, the Commission, the different components of the Parliament itself, not to speak of political forces and institutions within the States. While this study has concentrated on the role of Parliament, the building of a Community based on parliamentary democracy involves other institutions, the role of which in relation to the Community is no less in need of applied research—above all the role of the Commission as an executive authority, the continuing development of inter-governmental procedures in and around the Council, and the evolution of European political parties and interest groups. In fact, it is essential in considering the future role of the Parliament to have a view of the Community Institutions, and of the process of government in the Community, as a whole, bearing in mind the Community's basic principles and aims. To the extent that these differ from what we are accustomed to in the States, then we must avoid jumping to conclusions about the role of political institutions in the Community based on our limited, and for the most part disappointing, national experience.

Finally, therefore, the study has sought to stress the need to look at experience wider than that of the Community's Member States and wider than Western Europe, and to attempt a more ambitious approach to the theory of parliamentary democracy than has become customary when dealing with national parliaments in Europe. In these respects, the directly elected European Parliament promises to be an exciting subject for students and practitioners alike. It is not a subject only for those interested in European integration, and it is one that holds out far more possibilities than either the existing legal provisions or the current political discourse of the Community might otherwise suggest. Whether the promise is fulfilled, however, will depend on what practical men do with the new opportunity.